WILTSHIRE TIME CAPSULE

Wiltshire Time Capsule

Life in our County at the Turn of the Century

Edited by John Chandler, Roger Jones,
Mike Marshman and Linda Matthews

EX LIBRIS PRESS
in cooperation with
WILTSHIRE LIBRARIES AND HERITAGE

Published in 2000 by
EX LIBRIS PRESS
in cooperation with
Wiltshire Libraries and Heritage
1 The Shambles
Bradford on Avon
Wiltshire

Printed in England by
Cromwell Press
Trowbridge
Wiltshire

ISBN 1 903341 02 7

Wiltshire
COUNTY COUNCIL
EDUCATION & LIBRARIES

Index of Places and Contributors

Crockerton, Warminster	Mrs L Mae Harry	61
Crudwell, Malmesbury	Dave Bailey	14
	Evelyn Williams	155
Dauntsey	Felicity Hill	64
Devizes	Katherine Burbeck	22
	Jack Nichols	107
	Peter Stokes	144
Dilton Marsh	Roy Gregory	53
	Sean Kerwin	79
	Rebecca McKee	91
	Fiona Waite	152
Donhead St. Andrew	Hazel Hinchley	65
Durrington	Leigh Crabtree	36
Easterton, Devizes	Imogen Brown	18
	Paul Snook	139
Enford, near Pewsey	Dominic Mundy	106
Firsdown	Fenella Kennedy	77
Great Bedwyn, Marlborough	David Kershaw	78
Great Cheverell, Devizes	Gary Pike	113
Great Somerford, Chippenham	Jean Hopkins	67
Hullavington	Margaret Roberts	128
Limpley Stoke, Bath	Adam Kington	79
Little Somerford	Gordon Sharp	136
Lyneham	Christopher Diston	39
Maiden Bradley, Warminster	Rosie Brown	21
Malmesbury	Stuart Gilchriest	45
Marlborough	Laura Hues	69
	Mary E Powell	118
	William Spray	140
Melksham	Lisa Benham	17
	Danny Lucas	89
	Thomas Minshull	97
	Jake Sturgess	147
Netheravon, Salisbury	Mayley Mountjoy	105
Nettleton	Mrs Peter Olver	109
Newton Tony, Salisbury	Tony Lyons	90
Norton, Malmesbury	June Badeni	13
Norton Bavant, Warminster	Veronica Burden	23

Life at the turn of the century

Introduction

The end of a century and, especially, a millennium causes people to both look back into the past and look forward into the future. Not too many people are concerned about the present unless it is to compare it with past, future or both. In 1998 I was conscious of the activity in many Wiltshire parishes who were planning to research, write and publish a millennium book. Nearly all these books would be histories and I fell to thinking that it would be useful to record some aspects of present day life. We live in an age when more and more areas of our life are recorded than ever before; official forms, censuses, electoral registration, school records, health records, credit ratings, CCTV, business transactions, and so many more. What was left that was not being recorded in some way? Ordinary everyday life seemed to be the answer, what a previous generation might have termed 'country contentments' So was born the 'Your Life in Wiltshire' competition, open to everyone either living, working or in full time education in the Wiltshire County Council area.

We asked for essays of up to 500 words, up to 400 words from young people, on some aspect of life in Wiltshire. There was an enthusiastic response and we found that many schools also set the project as class work. We asked for material to illustrate the life, feelings and experiences of people in Wiltshire towards the end of the second millennium. The emphasis was on ordinary life, not events that will be preserved in newspaper files, but life as it is lived by most people for most of their lives. This is the type of record we would now find invaluable had it been created in the past so, in the manner of laying down wine or planting oaks for future generations to enjoy, we decided to establish an archive for our successors.

Many hundreds of entries were received and every one has been placed in this archive in the County Local Studies Library at Trowbridge and they are available for anyone who wishes to read them. Demand will not be great at first, but in 20, 50 and 100 years time this material, doubtless then in electronic form, will be well used by anyone who wants to discover what local life was like all those years ago. From these entries the judges, Linda Matthews, Roger Jones, John Chandler and myself, have selected 123 for this book which will be the published record of everyday life as experienced by Wiltshire people in 1999.

A wide range of themes and activities is covered in these writings but there are some subjects common to many. In the writings of younger people there is considerable concern for the environment; a concern which will benefit our county and country when they are older. We also found that many former service families returned to live in the county in which they were once stationed, as they liked it so much, and nearly everyone who entered liked living in Wiltshire and did not want to leave it.

Many writers expressed their appreciation of Wiltshire's scenery, the rolling downs, Salisbury Plain and the vales and valleys, but what also emerged was the depressed state of farming and the disappearance of village post offices and other rural services. Writings from farmers and their families showed just how low prices are for the producer in our apparently prosperous county which, only 200 year ago, had an economy based largely on farming. Most people also liked living in our one city and our towns. The towns fared particularly well with good use being made of local shops, sporting and cultural facilities and local clubs and societies.

Nowadays few people keep diaries, other than for appointments. We do not have the time to record the happenings of our day and our thoughts on the world around us as some people did in a more leisured, past, age. Home videos will show certain events in the life of a family but, those that survive, will not give too much more information than has been provided by photographs for the last 150 years. With all the technology at our everyday disposal we should be able to provide an important and lasting record for our descendants. Television touches on this with 'fly on the wall' documentaries and video diaries but one is always left with the feeling of how genuine can anyone be when they know that they are being filmed. It seems to be in writing that we come closest to expressing our true feelings and are able to provide an account of our activities that is not improved a little for the benefit of the listener or viewer. Maybe when we have written about ourselves we can stand back and view it dispassionately; it no longer seems so personal to us when it is in print.

It is interesting to imagine what people a hundred years hence will make of the writings collected in this book and in the archive. Will everything be totally foreign to them or will there be activities and feelings that they can respond to from personal experience? We do not really know but the very existence of these writings will show them how their ancestors lived, what they thought about and how they felt about a range of issues.

Publication of this material is very important and we are very grateful to Roger Jones and Ex Libris Press for taking on this book. A host of records, both national and local, will survive but few of these will be written by you and me about our commonplace activities and thoughts. We appreciate the efforts of all those who took part in the competition, not just those whose entries are published here, for in the future all your accounts will be valuable to researchers.

Michael Marshman

North Wiltshire, where I was born and have lived the greater part of my 74 years, is quite different from the south. Instead of Salisbury Plain, thatched cottages and huge tracts of arable land, we have the Cotswold stone with which our houses are built, our roofs tiled and our fields divided, dairying land and the heavy soil of the Dauntsey Vale. The small village of Norton has changed very little. Our tiny church struggles to survive with a congregation, usually, of five people. Our pub, The Vine Tree, has become less of a pub and more of an eating place, as have most pubs because of the drink/driving laws. The bus that used to come once a week comes no longer and is not much missed as every house has a car.

Our bird population has diminished dreadfully. Few skylarks, few thrushes, no spotted flycatchers which used to nest on the house from as long ago as I can remember until three years ago.

Looking forward from the threshold of the new millennium, one wonders how the future will look. Less birds? More cars? Heavier pollution? Fewer wild flowers? In my childhood we picked huge bunches of primroses in Leigh Delamere Wood to pack into shoe boxes with damp moss and send someone who was ill and our picking left no sign of depletion. Now, in order to prevent extinction of flowers that have become so scarce, it has been made an offence to pick them.

I remember when cars were so few that the children could safely play hopscotch and spin their tops on the road. Now, because of traffic and crime, no-one can let their children play in the road or wander unaccompanied over the fields.

With the highly mechanised farming of today, farms which used to employ four or five men now employ one or two. So the cottages which housed agricultural workers have now been smartened up and are occupied by people who work in Swindon or Bristol. The continuity of families where the young generation married and stayed in the village has gone. Even in the villages where a lot of new houses have been built, there are very few starter homes so the young people have to move away.

The extended family, where most young couples had parents and brothers and sisters nearby, is now very rare so the 'closeness' of a village has diminished.

When those imagined people read this a hundred years hence, it is impossible to forecast how they will see our Wiltshire. Perhaps – and God forbid – they will look back from a world without birds or wild flowers or stable families, with disease multiplying because of pollution and the country lanes closed with giant vehicles, and will see *our* world as a secure haven vanished forever. But perhaps – God willing – they will see it as the turning point where we glimpsed the horrors that *might* happen and began to build a world less polluted, chemically and morally, for them to enjoy.

Dave Bailey

I live in the village of Crudwell, only one mile from the border with Gloucestershire. My wife Lesley and I moved here in 1983 from Highworth, but prior to that we lived in Manchester. Personal mobility and a change of job allowed this move from a major industrial city to a rural village, a decision we have never regretted.

There are three of us now (our son Paul was born in 1991) and Crudwell is a delightful place for a family to live. When we were buying our house the estate agent described it as being 'on the edge of the Cotswolds', which may be an exaggeration, but Crudwell is pretty enough and, more than that, it is a working village. It has a school, a church, a garage, a shop and post office, two pubs and two hotels. It is a thriving community with a new village hall, financed by locally raised funds, at its heart. It has maintained, and long may it continue to do so, a proper balance between development to meet the needs of immigrants (like us) and the conservation of its village character.

My work base is Swindon. My employer, Castrol, was one of the pioneers in the 1970s trend for companies to move out of the crowded, expensive cities. The (then) ultra-modern headquarters building was described as 'A Place in the Country' in an attempt to persuade employees to make the move from central London to Wiltshire. Almost thirty years on, perhaps the days of such large corporate headquarters are numbered as it becomes increasingly possible to work from home, or indeed anywhere where a laptop computer and telephone link are available.

My own situation, working in the international division of a multinational company, means I am in the Swindon office for not much more than half my working year. Most of the rest of the time I spend travelling around the Asia Pacific region, an immense triangle with India, Japan and New Zealand at its extremes. This is not as romantic as it sounds as business travel is largely made up of a string of airports, aeroplanes, lookalike hotel rooms and meetings in offices. Nevertheless, these are exciting destinations and an occasional day off to explore them is a welcome privilege.

Because I visit such far flung places and am able to make comparisons, I really do appreciate what our country has to offer. At the risk of cliche, there really is no place like home and it is always a pleasure to return to my family, Crudwell and Wiltshire.

Kevin Baker

• •

A typical Saturday in my life at the dawn of the millennium starts with a cooked breakfast consisting of crispy bacon, delicious sausages, fried eggs and baked beans topped with tomato sauce. Then, after a cool shower, I sit and listen to some of my favourite CDs.

In the afternoon, I'll either load up a game on my Playstation or just sit with a cup of hot chocolate in the peace and quiet reading a classic children's book. At the moment I'm reading a Robert Westall book; I prefer children's books as they are often brilliantly crafted with a refreshing lack of cynicism and violence.

It is nice and peaceful in our old cottage. The thick Georgian walls block out any unwelcome noise from neighbours. It's solidly built and has character, unlike contemporary houses with their thin walls that spring up everywhere from increasing urban sprawl.

Occasionally I'll flick through Ceefax on my TV. That way I can read a balance of good and bad news. The newspapers and TV news just seem to dwell on the bad news, with a little bit of good news slotted in amongst the bad news if they have the room and the time. However, I'm concerned about the Kosovo refugees, so I like to keep up to date with what's going on. I don't watch much television so it wouldn't be worth my while subscribing to Sky TV or Cable TV.

If the weather's right I'll go out with my wife for a nice cold pint of Guinness in a pub beer garden, then have a couple of games of pool. We feel quite unique being married in our twenties, as marriage is not as popular as it used to be. Then, we'll maybe go for a drive down to the coast where we'll eat fish and chips with extra salt and vinegar whilst sitting on a sea wall overlooking the sea.

We own a Mini Cooper which is really fun to drive; it's a shame they are phasing out old-style Minis after the millennium. We like Minis because they were designed by hand instead of using computers and a wind tunnel. These cars have character, unlike a lot of present-day cars which all seem to look the same.

In the evening we'll come home to feed the cat. I'm allergic to our cat so it has to sleep in the hallway. Allergies and asthma are common ailments with people at this point in time. We usually visit friends or family in the late evening where I usually bring round a couple of bottles of my home-made wine.

I feel lucky to have my weekends free as there is an increasing trend towards working unsociable hours. A lot of my friends and family work night shifts or double day shifts making it difficult to meet up with them. This makes the time I do manage to spend with my family and friends even more valuable.

Lisa Benham, age 11

I was born in Trowbridge. I lived in Melksham, then moved to Bowerhill, which was still in Wiltshire. Where I live there are lots of dens. I have lots of friends where I live. I go to Forest and Sandridge School. It has a playground and playing field with a wooden playground.

If I had a chance to live in the city I won't, I like the cows and bulls and mole hills, I like to walk my dog in the field. I hope they won't build houses on it. I like Wiltshire. My best hobby is bike riding, there are lots of places to ride too! There are lots of birds. I wouldn't like to live in the city.

Chaz Blake, age 13

I have lived in Amesbury for seven years and a lot of changes have taken place. Amesbury is a large town near Stonehenge, but it's not very well known. I think it should be, because interesting things happen. I mean, who has Sting living down the road from you, or a 93 year-old woman committing suicide?

The village itself has changed a lot. The cinema was bulldozed and a corner shop has changed at least five times. The park was vandalised so they had to put a load of new rides in. An old shop got knocked down and turned into a bus stop. So it's quite a groovy, modern village.

It's good living near Stonehenge, for some reason it makes you proud. On the news you hear riots have broken out at Stonehenge and you think, hey! cool, I live just down the road from there.

Amesbury is quite relaxing and peaceful but not much happens. It's a nice village but a few things spoil it. Grumpy Grannies and common townies.

They sit around the bus stop all day, smoking, drinking and swearing. Something should be done about it.

Overall, Amesbury is a great town and I've enjoyed it in my seven year stay there.

Imogen Brown

● ●

Home: I live with two men (my father and my partner), two cats, Tango and Shadow, and a tank full of tropical fish. The overgrown garden is home to frogs, at least one toad, numerous birds, at least 20 native trees, diminishing numbers of moles, voles and mice (bad cats!), innumerable insects (which seem to live on vegetables intended for our kitchen) and a beautiful lizard. The house is approximately four hundred years-old and situated on the northern edge of Salisbury Plain on a no through road; we are lucky to experience little road traffic. However, at certain times it is very noisy – when the army's firing ranges are in use – then the windows and doors rattle in their frames, helicopters buzz about and tanks roar along the tracks. Sometimes at night the sky is lit up by flares.

Work: Mostly my work involves helping other people with their gardens. The battle with weeds is my bread and butter, although yesterday I spent the day in the kitchen preparing a meal for my other half's parents and grandparents. We are vegetarian; stuffed marrow with Linda McCartney's mince, roast new potatoes and beans from the garden followed by cheesecake with redcurrants and blackcurrants – yep, from the garden – and home-made ice cream; all of which seemed well received!

While gardening, I was fortunate enough to spend some time in the grounds of a local former iron works. I was filled with awe and primal fear to discover an adder one day whilst planting a tree. When not gardening or cooking, I spend some time making cards for sale; I am also trying to develop a board game.

Rest: I indulge in yoga; it is an excellent way to stop the mind's chatter.

I recently discovered 5 Rhythms dance; known as a moving meditation, which is great for bringing mind and body back together. We all seem to lead increasingly disjointed lives these days.

Play: We enjoy festivals, including the brilliant 26th Village Pump festival near Trowbridge, featuring the incredible Bob Geldof. It was an honour to be in the same field! Listening to music, live and recorded, and attempting to make our own also provide entertainment.

Years ago I went caving, climbing and canoeing and now I enjoy occasional horse riding and cycling, but mostly I prefer more restful pursuits, particularly reading, especially the works of Terry Pratchett (who lives in Wiltshire!) Bill Bryson (who I was delighted to meet) and Vernon Coleman, car lover and the voice of sanity in a mad world!

Today being 11 August 1999, eyes turned to the skies for the solar eclipse. I was fortunate to see it twice; once, waxing, through dad's ancient sextant and once on the wane, with my naked eyes. So I shall probably go blind tomorrow if you believe the experts!

The sky really did go eerily dark – a truly magical experience.

Maggi Brown

Half-way on the Sarsen Trail or the Wiltshire Marathon: The walkers are spread across the nastiest bit of the trail – the long, slow drag up to Redhorn. Slowly they move to the verges as we drive up. Feel ashamed: next time we'll carry a sign saying 'Refreshment Assistants' or some such! Arriving at the top, the eye takes in dozens of cars, scores of small, multi-coloured groups picnicking or resting, loos, Katie's Sandwich Bar, two ambulances and the large tent.

Inside the tent it is cool but the pace is hectic. Some walkers finish here, half-way on the trail, others plod on to Stonehenge. All have their sponsor cards stamped; those finishing receive a silver medal. Photos are taken. We at the drinks table try to keep up with the demand. We fill jugs from the bucket – Paul says, "Let me know when you want more water." The table is awash. We offer salt to anyone who looks as if they need it. A dog sticks its nose in the bucket – "Paul, more water." Out to the Army's bowser he goes and the jugs are refilled. The disposable cups are now being recycled "Paul, more water," as we start to rinse them.

And now the pressure is really on. Dusty shoes, swollen ankles, sweaty faces and such a variety of T-shirts: Greenpeace, Friends of the Earth, pop groups, holiday haunts and a couple of 'London Marathon 1990'! Some of the youngsters have personal stereos but no artificial noise is heard, only birds, laughter and talk. "This'll sound daft. I've done the first half, which way for Stonehenge?" We point him in the right direction – over the plain to the Bustard – "you might make it for opening time tonight!"

How many of them are there? Eight hundred and thirty were registered by this morning but there seems to have been more than a few late entries! "Paul, more water!" There's another hound at the bucket – put it inside a large cardboard box (the bucket not the dog!). The mobile phone rings – a casualty at Cannings Cross – someone's collapsed – with blisters! One of the St. John's teams leap with glee into their ambulance – at last, a job to do! These walkers are very well prepared.

And still they come, surely we must be near the end – what time did the last ones leave Avebury? The Army arrive early to collect their bowser – "Paul, water!" As they connect it up we fill all available containers; then, relentless, they tow it away.

Now it's only a trickle – walkers, not water! – we can knock off. Driving down the hill we pass only eight or nine people – surely the last! Must be busy at Stonehenge!

Bank Holiday tomorrow – time to rest those sore feet. I feel sorry for the dogs – they've no shoes and they've got *four* feet!

I am a farmer's wife living in the south-west corner of Wiltshire. The farm is 350 acres and is part of a larger estate. My husband runs a herd of Hereford x suckler cows, which are crossed with a Charolais bull. The calves are sold at nine months old to another farmer who fattens them to be sold as beef. Although the farm has been free of BSE, we hope that the market will improve when the export restrictions are lifted in August. We also rear lambs from Scotch mule ewes crossed with Suffolk rams and at lambing time produce up to a thousand lambs. They are fattened on the farm and ready for sale in July. This year the price has dropped considerably and we have applied to convert to organic meat production for both the beef and lamb. The farm struggles to make a profit and cannot support itself and our family.

We have two teenage daughters. They go to school in Shaftesbury and travel daily. I have a full-time job as a college lecturer, teaching business studies. I travel to work every day by car, driving fifty miles each day during term time. Last year I moved from teaching catering into business studies. I am studying a Higher National Certificate in Business Studies for two years and I have finished the first year.

I have a busy time during the weekends and holidays. We live in an old farmhouse and have a large flower and vegetable garden. I enjoy gardening and growing all the vegetables, soft fruits and flowers for the family.

We enjoy and take part in village life. I am a Parish Councillor and attend meetings to discuss various issues which concern and affect the whole village. For example, we are concerned about the amount of heavy traffic and the speed at which it drives through the main street.

The Village Produce Show and Fête held in August is a highlight of the village year. During the day we have various fun activities for all ages and in the evening a barbecue with live entertainment.

We have lots of friends in the village and surrounding area. We play bridge with friends and swim in the village pool. We attend services in Bradley Church, particularly Harvest Festival, Remembrance Sunday, Christmas Carols and Mothering Sunday. A flower festival is planned for July 2000, consisting of arrangements contributed by all the organisations and clubs in the village. There is a strong sense of belonging to a community and particularly the farming community as it goes back

several generations

My life is a balance between work, home, the farm and the village and I work hard to ensure our way of life will continue for generations to come.

Katherine Burbeck, age 13

You could say my life has been a bit unsettled. I was born in London General Hospital on the 17th of December 1985. When I was one and a half my parents moved to Oxfordshire. Then when I was three my parents divorced. This upset family life and a year later we moved to Sussex because my mother had been promoted. I spent three happy years there but we were then uprooted to Northamptonshire. We moved to a pretty house and I made many friends.

After two years my brother went to school in France and I was left alone with my mother. Halfway through the year my mother got promoted again to Wiltshire. By this time I was eleven and getting ready to go to senior school. I didn't want to start a new school for just one term. So it was decided I was to live with my father and go to school there for a term. My father had married and had a three year-old boy. I enjoyed this time. When at last my time was up, I came to Wiltshire.

It was strange and scary at first. I was going to go to Dauntsey's. This was my seventh school and I was petrified. When the term started I found out quite a few people didn't know anyone else and I soon settled in. After many arguments and pain I made five special friends who have stayed close for over a year now. I am nearing the end of my second year and feel I know this small friendly county quite well. I enjoy going riding and love to swim. We live in a beautiful house in Devizes. I know my way around town and enjoy shopping.

Wiltshire is one of the prettiest counties I have lived in. Although it is small it has all the facilities I need. I am going to stay at Dauntsey's until I finish my A-levels, which is settling for me. I have relaxed and I am doing well at school. I think moving here was a very good idea.

The only hope I have for Wiltshire is that the countryside does not disappear and get converted into ugly buildings like so much of England. Please don't ruin it for later generations.

Veronica Burden

I awake to the sound of the birds and the cock crowing. I can hear the distant rumble of the early morning traffic on the by-pass. The trains making their way to Salisbury and beyond make little echo on the track; this is my barometer – no rain today.

I quickly rise. The goat is bleating, come, see my beautiful coat, the linseed growing in the adjoining field is very good and makes it shine. The old family pony neighs in recognition of my appearance; Corby waits patiently for her ration of early morning fodder. Changes in farming have meant that more grazing is available for ponies to graze and lush pastures bring pain to the ponies' hooves and holes to the owners pockets as vets bills continue to rise. I can now access an individual land worker, using his own equipment, who will come and make the hay from the pastures, cut and treat the pastures as needed. Hay works out at 78 pence a bale. Caring for the field animals is much easier since the Water board has taken on the cottage water supply. Water pipes alongside separate field meters logging the water used removes the nightmare of carrying buckets yet brings with it the potential for mindless vandalism of the taps and troughs.

The hen houses are alive with their cries; corn mixed with oyster shell and layers of pellets are placed out in bowls, water buckets washed and filled and the great race begins. The blend of bantams and hens rush to take the first bite. The two Black Rock hens purchased four years ago as day-olds, always hit the food bowls first. Many of the old breeds of chicken are coming back and sell for anything from five pounds to twenty-five pounds. Eggs are collected morning and night – only five today so far; these will be used for cooking omelettes and a weekend cake for the family of six.

The wild bird numbers are changing nationally but I can still enjoy many wonderful sightings. Just a few weeks ago I saw a pair of buzzards attacking the tops of the big round bales in the field beyond us. Up the lane, in one of the distant cottages, there lives a falconer who enjoys leisure time flying his birds. Daily I can see the woodpeckers, both the lesser and greater spotted. The range of cousins from the tit family, sparrows, blackbirds, sometimes a thrush, the many barn and tawny owls hoot at night. The whole range of finches visit daily, goldfinches more often in winter and spring, jackdaws live in the beech tree up the lane, racing pigeons often drop in for a rest, the last one had a wound on its leg but it managed to move on after a week. The bullfinch is missing and I have not seen one for many years. The cuckoo came in May this year and stayed only a short while; the swallows returned in early April and are busy rearing their second family.

I am really lucky to live where I do, three miles from the centre of Warminster, yet our track is used only for farm vehicles, our two cars and visitors or walkers passing by the gate. Warmer winter months mean the last time we were snow-bound was 1981, the first year we arrived. Rain can be a problem with the rough track, yet to put a tarmac coat on would cost £10,000 and potentially spoil the natural beauty that is all around me. Stoats, the kingfisher and water rats down by the river, evening-time bats, dragonflies and stag beetles all delight my life. The five foxes growing into adulthood take an evening stroll through the newly harvested field. They seem to know that the life of the huntsman chasing them is nearing its end, for the last five years the horns and hooves have been missing from this local scene, the locals farmers will not have them on their land. Up on the road the cars still fly along even though the bypass is in action, a short cut always appeals to drivers, who have little thought for wildlife or rural residents. Whilst taking the horse and buggy out through the local B-roads or across Salisbury Plain, it is so sad to see the carnage of young animal life, birds, badgers, pheasants, foxes and deer. Why does our society feel the need to rush around?

Hello, I'm going to tell you what it is like to live in Wiltshire. First of all, I'm going to tell you what I usually do at weekends. On Saturdays I go shopping, mostly I go to Somerfield. In there you can get vegetables, fruit, cheese, meat, cold drinks, flour, sugar, pasta, teabags, sweets, crisps, cakes, cereal, bread, burgers, peas, soups, soaps, shampoo, conditioner and lots of frozen things. There are also two other supermarkets which sell the same items, they are called Kwik Save and Sainsburys in Calne. There are other shops in Wiltshire though.

The Library from Calne has different books, like fiction or non-fiction. It is opened at certain times so then anyone, anyday, can go to the Library easily. The people inside are called librarians. It is very nice to sit down and read a book without being interrupted. To take some books home you need a membership card, you can have them up to three weeks, you are allowed up to eight books.

On weekends it is a great time to go around and visit friends and family. There are loads of places to go swimming – to learn, play, compete or just to watch. If you look around Wiltshire you would be able to see quite a few pubs. In the pub you can have drinks, food or just sit down and have a good old chat. There is always a playground and toilets. If you like to play archery, Wiltshire is a good place to find loads of courses, archery is where you have a bow and arrow and shoot at fake animals. You can go to the toilet at archery in toilets that are easily moved, they look like plastic boxes which can go in caravans. In towns near shops there are always toilets, just in case, all over Wiltshire.

TV in Wiltshire has loads of things to watch, you can watch soaps, cartoons, drama and tragedies. In Wiltshire there is a radio station and you can listen to music, competitions and jokes. Wiltshire has some nice places to ride a bike or play with friends or even take your dog for a walk. At school there are loads of subjects including PE. After school you could go to netball or choir. You have homework every week at my school. During school on Tuesdays I play the Tenor Recorder. Or after school you can just sit back and read a newspaper about Wiltshire.

Well that's all, and I hope you have learnt a bit more about the 20th century.

W. Peter Carpenter

The Allotment of Space and Time! In our particular part of rural Wiltshire there is an increased interest in allotment gardening. A few years ago the number of us engaged in this particular activity had dwindled to only four. Various coinciding factors brought about this situation. Three of the allotmenteers moved away from the area; one exchanged his terrestrial plot for a celestial one; two retired because of age and infirmity; and three were given notice because of encroaching housing development. In consequence of this, the vacant plots were soon to become jungles of weeds. It is gratifying to report that the number of active allotment tenants has now grown to twelve. What is also interesting and rather surprising is that five of these are young people, three are in the forty/fifty age group, whilst the remaining four of us are pensioners.

Unlike the carefully managed sites in the larger towns and cities which are fenced in, have properly laid out watering systems and, in some places, tool sheds, ours is just an open area roughly divided into plots. These vary in size but average out at about thirty yards long by ten yards wide. The only facility that we have is one water tap on the far side of a small car park.

The vacant plots are mown monthly on a Parish Council contract and one vacant plot is kept rotavated for immediate tenancy as and when required.

The soil is a medium to heavy neutral loam on a sandstone ridge. It is quite productive but requires a regular 'load of muck'. With a farm close by this is no problem. Unfortunately the site is largely open to the cold north and easterly winds and is therefore not the best situation for early sowing as the cold soil inhibits germination of the seeds. During a prolonged spell of wet weather the soil does tend to compact and working it down into a fine tilth can sometimes become rather difficult.

There is a public footpath along the north-west boundary but because we are unfenced people use the allotment paths as a short cut to the school and sports centre. In spite of this we thankfully get very little vandalism or theft. As in most places, we do get plant damage from pigeons and other birds if we fail to use appropriate protective measures.

Allotments were originally small plots of land where the poorly paid working class could grow vegetables essential for the feeding of the family. Nowadays most people of all classes prefer to buy from the supermarkets. Today the allotmenteers come from various walks of life, and we all rub shoulders in that common interest and pastime; sharing our knowledge and experience; comparing the performance of different varieties; swapping plants; congratulating success; commiserating over failure; finally, in total agreement that vegetables fresh from the allotment have the finest flavour!

Jonathan Carter, aged 10

My name is Jonathan Carter, I am just over ten years-old. I'm here in Winterslow to tell you about my wonderful Wiltshire life. I am pleased to live in the peaceful Gunville Road. I live in a modern, two-storey house, and yes, you guessed it, it's named Gunville House! (Why are people like that when it comes to house names!) The only downside to Gunville Road is the traffic. It's not much but from all the lorries it is quite a bit of noise. I'm not complaining, but it is.

I like the bus service, it is good that they think of family and friends. I would definitely like to see the service carrying on because they put the buses at times when my friends can come to Salisbury with me.

My best friend James Glover (who lives next door) and I have the same interests and we have a particular favourite — football! Luckily we have a brilliant football club in the village and the community has helped to build it up to something that is regular. We play on the recreation ground where there is a pitch that we use when we sometimes invite other villages over for a match.

The community is small but is effective and helpful. The school, for example, is only kept going by the community who are always coming up with great ideas. In fact, right now, some of the community are constructing a conservation area.

The church is a nice place to go if you would like a nice peaceful time with your family. The church is a whole different place to go to because all the people who go there like to worship together and are very nice towards each other. The rector and the congregation are willing to help you with any problems you may have, I always look forward to Sundays because there is Junior Church. I like Junior Church because it is fun but you learn at the same time.

I like Winterslow because of the beautiful countryside that surrounds it. There are lots of walks I have not yet explored.

That is basically my life in Wiltshire. But there is one thing I'm dying to tell you about, the ice-cream man!

Jim Caslaw

A Generation in Purton Stoke, 1969-1999: My wife, two young sons, and myself arrived in Purton Stoke at the end of the 1960s. In one generation we have seen the village change and grow.

There are 67 houses now in our village, and 18 of those were built during those years. They are: 39 detached houses, 4 terraced cottages, one of which used to be the post office and shop, 16 semi-detached houses, seven farm houses and yards, only three of which are now used for farming, one public house, one Primitive Methodist chapel, a derelict spa and one former school building that is now a horticultural learning centre for mentally disadvantaged young adults. Three of the houses are second homes. The pub has seen seven changes of landlord.

The village is compactly built and surrounded on all sides by fields stretching for two miles to the north, east and south before meeting the urban housing of Cricklade, Swindon and Purton. To the west lies rural Wiltshire for many more miles. From my upstairs window I can see nine new, brick, detached 4/5 bed-roomed houses that have been built in the last few years replacing an old stone farmhouse, cottage, orchard and barn. I still have a mental picture from a few years ago of a cow poking her head through a hole in the side of the hundred year-old barn.

The village is still surrounded by fields with cows, but sheep are also being raised now, and the occasional arable crop or turf field appears as well. Horse riding as a leisure interest is leading to many of the fields being taken over as paddocks, and stable blocks are being built.

The River Key and bridge are still there of course, but the Spa Lane bridleway is now covered in tarmac. Large vegetable gardens have given way to patios, paving, lawns and shingle. The school and shop were closed, and mains sewerage and a pumping station were introduced during those years.

Every day during the summer months, the farmers still take their cows to and from the milking parlours, using the main street. Sheep are taken to fresh fields from time to time. Horses clip-clop their way slowly through the village. Wild deer make brief appearances. The Hunt gathers in the winter-time, and the varied collection of horses, riders and hounds pursue some of the many foxes that live around the village.

When we arrived more people were around during the day, and they met and talked in the village shop, school and the pub. Women were mostly at home looking after their children. Buses were frequent and there were regular deliveries of milk, bread, fish, vegetables, etc.

The flagging community spirit received a boost in 1977 with the Jubilee celebrations. The whole village enthusiastically joined in the sports, football matches, a parade, a tug-o-war over the River Key and a village feast at the end of the day. Because of this renewed feeling, in 1979 a village committee was formed to organise events throughout the year and raise funds to give the over-60s a traditional Christmas dinner and the under-16s a special treat too, such as a party or a pantomime trip. The fund continues to exist, and new families are encouraged to participate. We have many proposals in hand to celebrate the Millennium year.

When we arrived we were new villagers. Most of the existing ones could trace connections with others in the village. Forty-nine new families have come into the village in the years since we arrived, some of these replacing other new families, who only stayed for a while. It is now truly an urban village. Only thirteen of the original families remain, with five of their next generation owning houses here. We remain too, but our sons live and work in London.

I retired from farming and came to live in Whiteparish in 1986. However, I am not alone in doing that. Over the last fifteen years a fair number of people have come to live in the village. As far as my wife and I were concerned the place had everything we needed to have a comfortable retirement. A rural atmosphere, yet within easy reach of other towns and motorways. Unlike other villages we considered this parish had a feeling of life throbbing vigorously as we had been used to in our farming days. It also had a surgery and four pubs – what more could one ask! A church and chapel made sure of the other spiritual needs.

Now it is July 1999, and the life of the village is changing rapidly, but in our opinion not for the better. Well, we feel for the future of all the activities that exist within the village. Church, Chapel, Garden Club, Youth Club, Scouts and Guides, Women Institute. Even the Village Hall. Those of us who have reached the age when it is more than time to give up active work in any of these organisation, are finding it very difficult to do so. Why? Well, no one of the younger generation wants to take over. They say when asked if they would like to be a secretary or treasurer that they wouldn't know how to do the job, or they have not got the time. Family life and work to pay the mortgage are the reasons frequently given. No one it would seem wants to take any responsibility, even after fifty years of vastly improved education. But then perhaps times have begun to change – these activities are no longer as important as we once thought. The time is perhaps coming that needs only a vast communication network and a computer to make social life complete. That, together with the public houses of the village which are indeed now the focal points for conversation.

As far as we are concerned we still enjoy our Garden Club and the chance to meet others, hand-bell ringing, running a local pheasant shoot and recently formed History and Environmental Club. Unfortunately most of those who have joined are getting on in years. During the years we have lived in the parish the farming has changed. Much of the land which used to be attached to one holding has been sold off in bits and pieces, and the number of chaps who used to work the land have gone. It smacks of a return to the farming depression of the days of our youth. To us it means the underlying throb of life in the parish has got a very weak pulse. Will it recover in the new millennium?

Rowan Cherrington

Chute Forest was never a village but a parish, based on the old Chute Lodge estate. When my wife and I moved here in 1959, it was a working parish with five farms, four of whom ran diary herds, and a boys' prep school, 'Staddles', occupying the big house, and holding services in the estate church. I had taken over the running of the Home Farm and at that time employed four men, and at least twelve children were taxied to the local village school and the same number to Marlborough Grammar School or to the Secondary Boys' and Girls' schools in Ludgershall. We were never big enough to have a pub or a village shop, or even a public telephone box, depending instead on our neighbouring village of Lower Chute. We had a weekly bus service and twice a week a butcher and a baker called and groceries could be delivered from Andover or Ludgershall. At that time we did not have a Parish Council but a Parish meeting. For ten years I was Chairman of that meeting. However in the early seventies a Parish Council was formed.

Now, forty years later, my wife and I are the longest surviving inhabitants of the parish. No longer is it a largely agricultural working parish, just a scattered settlement of householders most of whom work well away from the village and in some cases away from Andover, our nearest town. There is no public transport, no baker or butcher calls, although two milkmen deliver. The estate church is now officially redundant, with one service being held there annually. No children go to the local village school in Upper Chute as that too has been closed. In fact there are very few children in the parish. Home Farm Chute Lodge is no more, as I sold it to my neighbours three years ago and they in turn sold off the farmyard to the new owner of the old farmhouse so there is no farm centre any more. During the week and indeed during the weekend the whole hamlet seems to be deserted.

The above paragraph sounds very depressing but life for us is still varied. The changes that have occurred to Chute Forest will have only mirrored changes that have taken place in hamlets and villages all over Wiltshire. We depend on being a part of the larger community. Chutes too have changed but the community spirit of the village is alive and kicking. The old school house is now the Village Hall run by a very enthusiastic chairman and backed by a hard working committee. There are various clubs in the village although sadly the Chute Women's Institute is in the process of winding up. The annual fête, still recognised as one of the best in the area, is held every June on our well maintained Playing Field. Gardening Club, Mothers and Toddlers, the Wednesday Club, Dancing Clubs, Bridge Club and others all make the Chutes a pleasant place to live. A 'Link' scheme, has been established. And all the time we have our glorious scenery in a lovely part of Wiltshire. I for one would never leave Chute Forest willingly but hope to be carried out in a box.

Hannah Clarke, aged 10

I am a very unusual 10 year-old girl, because I don't mind getting dirty and I don't care what I look like. I quite enjoy company from other people although I would rather be mucking out stables.

The community is very friendly as I discovered when a surprise house-warming party was held in our next door neighbour's garden only two days after we moved in. The school is very friendly, and I have made good friends with Tammy my riding teacher as well as Obe and Jefro, two ponies at her riding school.

My hobby is riding horses, I enjoy this a lot because every time you walk into the yard something different is going on, you can never predict what the horse will do or if it's in a good mood or not and also because every ride is different and a challenge.

My antics with horses and adventure often get me into a muddle. When I was six I broke my leg having a tug-o-war with my best friend, and now after flying over the handlebars of my bike am recovering from a badly broken arm.

I enjoy my home life a lot and if I'm not around and not down at the local riding stables I'll be reading a book or drawing animals in my bedroom.

I like Wiltshire as a county because it is friendly and there is lots of countryside, although I do think we should try and cut pollution levels more.

Reginald Coole

'Tomorrow and tomorrow and tomorrow Creeps in this petty pace from day to day To the last syllable of recorded time.'

In his play 'Macbeth' Shakespeare expresses the lifestyle of many who have been fortunate to spend their lives in a Wiltshire country town. Cricklade is such a place, not unlike others in the county. There is an atmosphere of timelessness which still pervades the ancient streets and buildings of the old centre of the town. Our history dates from King Alfred, who fortified this settlement to protect his Saxon Kingdom against marauding Danes, crossing the River Thames to pillage and rob. We still have his 'grid pattern' of roads, and until recent years most of the town was contained within Alfred's town walls. About sixty Cricklade coins still exist, minted here (marked 'CREC' or 'CROC') before and during the Norman Conquest.

Nothing much of note then happened until the 18th century when Cricklade, a 'Rotten Borough', precipitated the beginnings of electoral reform. Cobbett in his *Rural Rides* was scathing: '1821, 7th November: I passed through that villainous hole, Cricklade... a more rescally place I never set eyes on.'

By contrast, small country towns, arguably, form the structures for the best communities today. We know well all our neighbours and have at least a nodding acquaintance with everyone else in the town. Family tragedies involve numerous offers of help and, being a closely knit community, crime rates are low. Of course, there are problems. So far we have managed to retain a few local shops, in spite of the proximity of supermarkets on the outskirts of nearby larger towns. We have no senior school and, from the age of 11 years, pupils are bussed in all directions to school elsewhere. We do have a small industrial estate, but most work in Swindon causing a daily procession of motor cars, mostly with a single occupant, and a resulting traffic jam. As a retired person I enjoy the luxury of being able merely to observe. Because Cricklade is an ancient borough we have no Mayor. Instead we have a High Bailiff, a time-honoured office, which I have the honour to hold at present. We have a Court Leet which meets from time to time. Although we appoint officers – Constable, Assayer, Ale-taster, Scavenger and so on – the only authority we retain is to supervise the pasturing of animals on North Meadow which forms 100 acres of Lammas Land, where townsfolk have rights to graze cattle and horses from August to February.

The twentieth century has seen enormous changes. We have literally moved from the horse and cart era to the computer and space age. We wonder, can the extent of man's knowledge continue to snowball at such a rate? Can the problems of small communities be solved without losing their individual identities? Perhaps, dear reader, you will have the answers!

Catherine Courtney

My first memory of Wiltshire is as a girl of twelve in the sixties, eating peanut butter sandwiches in a car in Savernake Forest. I was on a family holiday from Norfolk; rain streamed down the windscreen and I ached to jump out and explore the mysterious, beckoning forest.

I could hardly believe my luck when, fifteen years later, my husband, Frank, began a career as an education officer at County Hall, Trowbridge. We moved with our two small daughters from Manchester to Chippenham. Weekends became time for discovering the downs, neolithic barrows, villages of honey-coloured stone. Vincients Wood and adjoining Dragon Tooth Meadow where we watched little owls in the dusk were only a walk away.

We noticed rows of dead elms, killed by Dutch elm disease and were uneasily aware that many of the green spaces on the edge of town would disappear under concrete before the end of the century.

Claire and Rebecca settled happily into a routine of playgroup, expeditions to the fields to pick blackberries or the first hazel catkins, trips to the library or the open-air swimming pool in Monkton Park. On Sunday mornings we often attended the Quaker meeting in Bradford on Avon.

I surprised myself by passing the driving test and once the girls were at school I undertook sporadic employment as a home tutor for the local authority. It was varied and interesting work. My pupils, whom I taught in their own homes for ten hours a week, ranged in age from five to sixteen and reasons for being unable to attend school included illness, pregnancy, emotional and behavioural problems. Seventeen years later I still enjoy this work although now the pupils receive only four hours teaching a week.

At one stage when Rebecca was not thriving at primary school I decided to educate her at home for a while. It happened that I was tutoring another nine year old girl at the time and the two children relished their tiny class. They wrote and performed dramatic dialogues about fox hunting and protecting the environment.

There were other concerns which were too grim to burden children with. In the late seventies and early eighties the Cold War was at its height. The nuclear arms race seemed out of control. Deep under Corsham the 'Maggie' Bunker was prepared to shelter the Prime Minister and her war cabinet in the event of war. The public was told there would be a four minute warning before the bombs fell – nowhere near long enough to gather the family together.

I joined Chippenham CND and, along with many others, directed my nervous tension into demonstrations, leafleting and letter writing.

In the early eighties I used to wonder if our children would live to grow up. It is now 1999. Frank and I have a baby grandson. I am looking forward to taking him to pick blackberries in Vincients Wood.

I am presently twelve years old and nearly thirteen. I was born at Odstock hospital and lived in Amesbury for about nine months, after that my Mum, Dad and I moved to Durrington into a bigger house.

My brother Daniel was born five years after my birth. My parents decided with a new baby on the way we would have to move to another house with three bedrooms and a big garden for my Dad. This was fine except there was nowhere they could find with a big garden, so my parents decided to settle for a small bungalow along Bulford Road.

The bungalow was great, it had eight rooms, two detached. There was a bathroom, three bedrooms, a kitchen, a long hallway and a dining/living room. The garden was a bit messy to start with, however, it soon looked nice. The garden is very long.

My close relatives are my Nan and Grandad, my Mum and Dad, and my younger brother Daniel. The person out of these who understands my thoughts most is Daniel. He may only be eight but he sure is clever for a child of his age.

I don't have a proper pen pal, but I write to my Aunt. My Aunt isn't an old fogie, her name is Angela but she likes being called Angie. She thinks along the same wavelength as me, which means she's fun to talk to.

I have lots of friends at the school I go to now, but at my old school I used to have a best friend called Michael Bosley. We're still best friends now because we meet each other sometimes.

I go to Amesbury Stonehenge School even though I live in Durrington. The first school I went to was Durrington Infants, aged four and a half. After that I went to Durrington Junior School, which I live next door to.

When I'm older I want to work on aircraft as cabin crew leader. I'm learning Spanish and French. I like being around other people.

I also play the piano and I'm presently working on grade three theory and practical. I enjoy playing Disney music and jazzy pieces. I enjoy drawing and reading, comedy books are best. So this is my mark in history, all about me, Leigh Crabtree, hope you enjoyed it.

Home is in a little village tucked into the Salisbury Plain, with my mum, dad, three brothers, one dog, one cat, one rabbit and four guinea-pigs. Bratton is a small village near Westbury. I have people living all around me, which sometimes can get rather annoying because you can hear their music and their arguments, but living with neighbours all around you creates a friendly and close community.

The main advantage of living in Bratton is the long countryside walks with family and friends. On a Sunday afternoon, after a mouth-watering Sunday roast, we normally go on a walk. When you are at the top of the hill, you can see a bunch of buildings that make up Bratton. However, most importantly when you are at the top of the hill, there is a sense of space and freedom. This feeling is created by the lusciously long, free-flowing fields surrounding the village.

This sense of space is sadly disappearing. As I travel to different places in our car, it saddens me to see yet another housing estate being built over the top of what was once a timeless grassy field. There is no immediate way of stopping the houses being built because they are being built due to more divorces and population growth. No one can ultimately change these two facts from happening but what we can do is care about the hills and fields that are around us now.

In the future, I am going to make a difference, maybe not to lots of people. However, if I make a difference in just one person's life, then my life would have been worth living. Bratton is home and always will be, but for me to make a difference, I have to get out. My heart lies in the Third World countries like Africa. In February 1999, I visited Gambia. That trip has really made me determined. I am going to do my bit and make a difference in this dying world.

If we carry on treating the things around us the same, then sadly I am pessimistic about the twenty-first century. For my opinion to change, all that people have to do is their best. If we all do our bit then Wiltshire, and many other places, will be a place to be proud of.

I live in the north-west of Wiltshire in a small country village called Brinkworth. It is the longest village in England. My school is called Brinkworth Earl Danbys Primary School. It starts at 8:45 am and finishes at 3:15 pm. I go on the bus to and from school. I have school dinners and although a lot of children don't like them I do. My Mum and Dad are divorced and I live with my Dad and my step-Mum Liz. I see my Mum every other Sunday. My Mum is a nurse and works at Princess Margaret Hospital in Swindon. My step-Mum is a secretary/receptionist. My Dad hasn't got a job yet. My family mainly shop in Tesco but my Mum shops in Sainsburys.

I was born in Princess Margaret Hospital. I was nine weeks premature. I go to a dentist in Marlborogh and the doctors surgery in Wootton Bassett called Tinkers Lane Surgery. Every other Sunday I go to my Mum's house — she lives in Swindon. When I go to my Mum's we have Sunday lunch and go out to places like Coate Water Park in Swindon and Cotswold Water Park in Ashton Keynes.

I have a friend called Jade who lives about ten houses down the road from my house. I call for her after school and although she goes to secondary school we are still friends. When we see each other we listen to music, watch T.V., play on the computer, help each other with our homework and we are also both in the First Brinkworth Guides. My friends at school are Rebecca, Lauren, Zara and Emma. I also have a friend called Katherine who has moved to America but is coming back in June. They are all really good friends. Rebecca and I play the flute and clarinet. Rebecca is doing her grade 3 on her clarinet in the summer. I am doing my grade 4 in the summer. I go to Brinkworth Concert band. Rebecca is in the junior band and I'm in the senior band. I have lots of pets they are Ben the dog, Flopsy the rabbit and Marmaduke the cat. We also have six fish.

I have just done my S.A.T.s they were quite hard but they were alright. I have three sisters. One is my proper sister, the other two are my dad's first children. My proper sister is called Emma she is twenty in November, lives with her boyfriend Stuart and is a bank accountant. My half-sisters are called Caron and Shelly. I also have two step-brothers called Chris and Ian. My half-sister Shelly has two children who are my niece and nephew. My niece is called Jasmine and is three soon and my nephew is called Sam and is two months old.

Christopher Diston, age 10

I live in Lyneham. It is mostly quiet. To me it is like a village because it has got two shops, lots of houses. There are a lot of different shops like flower shops. I do not have any neighbours because I live on a farm. The nearest garage is very close but the nearest shop is about half a mile away. My Mum works with horses. She cleans them and rides them for a living. My step dad's tractors are Ford ones. On Monday, when it is a school day, I wake up at 7 o'clock as I always do. Then when I have got dressed I take my dog out, called Chances. When I am ready for school my step dad takes me to my Nan's house in Dauntsey. There I get on the bus to school. When I get to school I meet my friends. Then when it is work time I do my best most of the time. I try to answer questions as well as I can. When it is the end of the day I go with my mum to do the horses in Brinkworth. My best activity is football. At school it is PE. When we are working I like maths. My interests are animals because I like the way they move. When I am at school I have a best friend called Daniel. Daniel likes food, Land Rovers and Discoveries. When I am at home I have a brother called Phillip. He is 3 years old. I have a step dad because my Mum and Dad split up. My brother likes tractors because his Dad works on the farm. My Dad lives in Calne. I see him every weekend there. I have a sister called Joanna. She is 3 as well. My step mum is having another baby in September. My birthday is September. My dad likes football as I do, our favourite team is Swindon Town. The season has finished.

Unlike Stonehenge, that prehistoric outpost secluded from ongoing life, Avebury remains an occupied place. A landscape inhabited since before writing, before royalty, and before state interference. Having endured the influence of immediate human occupation, cohabitation with the stones is what has made Avebury the very core of history.

Paradoxically, prehistory has made Avebury a World Heritage Site, yet the prehistory visitors come to see was erected in the 1930s. English Heritage protects the site, yet the National Trust has orchestrated the destruction of many ancient cottages and other buildings. The neighbourhood's living memory is invaluable, yet the community has been transplanted as much by the heritage movement as by incomers inducing increased property prices. The native people thus remain dislocated from their school, shop, post office, garage, social club, sports field, village hall, pub, church, and chapel.

Where other Wiltshire villages no longer have such facilities, Avebury's exist because visitors bring trade and incomers patronise services ignored by longstanding residents. Trade is also buoyed by the caravan park, a motorbike club, and through traffic; all made unwelcome by locals who use pubs but do not use the Red Lion, or use the club but only go to church for nuptials and funerals.

Heritage status negates any sense of community by enforcing an unrealistic clinical feel, a sanitized uniform product and guaranteed expurgated creation, devoid of life and individual character. The organic nature has been so sterilised that Aubrey and Stukeley would not recognise the place. The traffic is similar, but the evidence of two millennia has been cleared whilst megaliths have magically appeared. Such is the change that the Avebury future generations will inherit is neither the creation of prehistoric peoples, nor of the indigenous community, but of the heritage industry.

An industry now guides half a million visitors seeking spiritual guidance, historic reason, cultural identity, or just occupying their children with a whiff of heritage whilst their dog relieves itself. The New Age traveller and the cereologist wander past the dormitory resident going line dancing in Marlborough leisure centre and the single parent wondering what to go without to buy a Lottery ticket. The lottery that keeps the heritage industry rumbling on.

Avebury plies us with images crowding our feelings, echoing greatness and a nation of one voice, whilst distorted historical perspectives send powerful messages overwhelming alternative lines of enquiry. The heritage landscape persistently remakes England, and preserves perceived unity through archetypal images and patriotic histories. Yet if we peer through the potpourri haze of Avebury, we glimpse the fragmented society which created and maintain the heritage landscape.

D. M. & G. M. Firmager

At the beginning of the twentieth century Semington was basically a farming community, with agricultural and related employment for about sixty people. A small country lane ran through the village, which was also fairly self-sufficient, having a baker, a couple of grocers and a market garden, a sub-postmaster, a blacksmith and a couple of pubs. The Melksham Union Workhouse, which in 1891 housed some 140 inmates, would have required some goods and services. There were flour mills on Semington Brook and the busy junction of the Kennet & Avon and Wilts & Berks canals saw a big passing trade in Somerset coal. Employment in the village in the 1990s is now limited to one public house, a post office/store, a motor sales business and a mere handful of people employed in farming, plus one or two jobs on the local mini-industrial estate. There were approximately sixty buildings in the village at the beginning of the century. This number has risen to nearly 350 towards the end of 1999.

The change really began in the second half of the century when farm machinery began to be introduced. This therefore reduced the working opportunities in the village and it became necessary for people to travel to their employment. This single factor marks the beginning of the transformation from an agricultural village, with people walking to work locally, to a commuter dormitory settlement, with some people travelling up to forty miles each way to and from their jobs in Swindon, Bath, Bristol, Chippenham, Salisbury, Westbury, Trowbridge and Melksham. At the beginning of the century the village inhabitants came from long-resident local families whose ancestors could be traced back over many years. The vast majority of the population now have originated from outside the county of Wiltshire, attracted by the local environment and proximity to some very beautiful scenery.

What had previously been a cohesive village unit has become a divided settlement split by the former Semington-Melksham lane, with its dry stone bridge over the Kennet & Avon Canal, being turned into a major road. Traffic which at the beginning of the century consisted of a few carts has risen to a high of over 2000 vehicles in one hour, causing the County Council to provide a light-controlled crossing to enable the residents of the two halves of the village to interact.

Looking to the future, it is envisaged that more people may be working from home on their computers, and as with so many small villages the little shop is likely to be under threat because of the way people tend to use supermarkets instead. Cars will still take precedence over public transport and virtually all the present residents believe that unless the promised by-pass becomes a reality very soon the amount of traffic on the A350 will make life intolerable.

We moved to Wiltshire in December 1981, and were lucky enough to find a house in the lovely village of Biddestone.

Now that we are both retired, our life revolves to a great extent round our two dogs. It is a joy to be able to walk them in the quiet lanes and fields within five minutes of our home, and in doing so we experience at first-hand the ever-changing countryside, seeing an amazing variety of wild flowers, and watching the growth of the crops throughout the spring and summer until the machines rumble in to harvest them. Crops seem to have become more colourful over recent years – not only the garish yellow oilseed rape but also the glowing, delicate blue linseed. We see wildlife too: hares, foxes, occasionally a small group of deer; and among the varied bird life: pheasants, yellow-hammers, flocks of lapwings, exultant skylarks and, perhaps most exciting of all, buzzards which soar and wheel effortlessly in the sky above the woods in the Bybrook Valley.

My interests in the village centre firstly around the church. My duties there have always been many and various, not only administration and pastoral work, but also taking part in services. This led to my being licensed in October 1998 as a Lay Reader, and I can now lead non-Eucharistic services and preach sermons, duties which I find enjoyable but also challenging. Our parish is part of a group of eight, and I could find myself helping out at any of those churches. I also help run a Bereavement Support Group.

Apart from the church, other village organisations with which I am involved are the Women's Institute, the Tennis Club and the Village Hall Committee. Whilst resisting serving on the W.I. Committee, I participate in its running to the extent of captaining the skittles team and occasionally acting as Delegate to County meetings.

I am fortunate enough at age sixty to be still playing tennis, and am a member of Biddestone Tennis Club. We play in the Chippenham & District League, with matches all over the area from April to August. I also play in a ladies foursome throughout the winter, and take part in local charitable tournaments.

Much of my time is spent on work for Biddestone Village Hall Committee, of which I am Secretary. We desperately need a Village Hall, especially now that the School has closed. We have been granted planning permission to rebuild the existing sports pavilion as a Village Hall/Sports Club, and are now applying for major funding from various bodies, principally the National Lottery. We also do a great deal of fund-raising locally, by such events as quiz evenings, concerts, safari suppers and sponsored walks. We hope that not far into the new millennium Biddestone will have a Village Hall to be proud of.

Living in this beautiful part of England at the end of the twentieth century is enjoyable, usually peaceful but never dull. I feel very fortunate to be here.

Tessa Frayling

Tracing my family history is a fascinating hobby. It has taken me around Wiltshire and beyond, meeting new friends and relatives from as far afield as America. I have travelled back in time to discover the lives of my ancestors.

I live in the Wiltshire town of Westbury, the Mason family arriving with the advent of the railway. My father sparked my interest in genealogy with boyhood tales: sitting astride the shires on uncle George's farm on the Plain, helping Uncle Frank tend his sheep on Upton Cow Down and of strange goings-on at Aunt Nellie's where ghostly figures would search for gold! Mother, too, would recount childhood tales – her mother was the youngest of a family of fifteen so no shortage of family adventures there.

I began my research by questioning my parents and surviving grandparents. How I wish I had recorded, by written word or tape, more of their wonderful stories as my grandparents have now gone, also sadly my father's memory. Other relatives have been most helpful, providing photographs, certificates and a family Bible. Having joined the Wiltshire Family History Society I began corresponding with a Scammell cousin from California, who has since visited my home.

One morning I took myself off to the County Record Office in Trowbridge, by lunchtime I had traced Mother's family – Mines – back to 1700 in the reign of Queen Anne! I discovered a wealth of social history; poverty, illness, war, notoriety – transportation for sheep stealing in 1817. I also found many happier events and more than a few surprises!

I have always been intrigued by stories of my paternal Great Grandmother – Mary Jane – rumoured to be of Romany stock. Perhaps explaining my family's interest in gypsy caravans and our swarthy looks. She married Eli Gilbert and here I drew a blank, until a telephone call from an unknown distant relative a year or so ago. I had been traced via a cousin still living in the cottage in the village of Stockton where Eli had lived – and died whilst singing 'Rock of Ages' in 1925. The 'phone conversation culminated in a family get-together with some of the thousand or so descendants of Edward Gilberd (1735-90). This time the research had been done for me.

My quest continues, hopefully aided by the computer delivered to my house today. I hope the knowledge gained will be passed on to my son, Rowan, and to any future generation. Who knows, *you* may be one of my descendants!

Stuart Gilchriest, age 15

My name is Stuart Gilchriest and I have lived in the tiny hamlet of Chedglow all my life. Chedglow currently has about fifteen houses in total, and is a part of the parish of Crudwell, a larger village on the main road from Malmesbury to Cirencester. I go to Wycliffe College School in Stonehouse, which is about 35 minutes away by road and 20 minutes by train from the nearest station, Kemble. I am currently taking 11 GCSEs, including Information Technology, French, German, Maths and Geography.

For leisure and recreation, I enjoy playing most sports, including cricket, golf, fishing, football and rugby. I am currently in the Gloucestershire under-15 cricket team, play for my village, and I am in many of the teams at school for football, cricket and rugby.

At home I live with my parents and younger brother, James, who is eight years old. I have three, much older adopted brothers who have all left home to pursue their respective careers. I adore living where I do, because it is quiet and secluded, but not cut off from outer civilization. The worst thing about living here for a teenager like me, is the fact that there is little public transport nearby and we rely on our parents too heavily to 'ferry' us around.

I enjoy seeing my school friends, but many of them live a long way away from me, and I have to go to Gloucester by train to see them. Therefore I do not get much time to meet people of my age in the village.

At the moment, there is a wonderful atmosphere in the village: everyone gets on with each other well and it is a place where everyone knows everyone else. We all enjoy the rural life of Crudwell and hope that it doesn't change too much in the next hundred years.

Judith Giles

I am woken by the alarm at 7.30am and immediately turn to look at my husband, who is recently home from Salisbury Hospice. He is suffering from lung cancer and after a single session of chemotherapy, mitomycin C, vinblastin and cisplatin being injected into his blood via his left hand, is now on palliative care.

A visiting nurse comes from Salisbury District Hospital once a week to see if *we* need help of *any* kind and our General Practitioner visits once a week to prescribe drugs and so today we can carry on with our lives.

I get up and prepare breakfast: cereals, toast, pills and water for Lee; museli, juice and tea for me; Lee's on a tray for the bedroom, mine for the dining room where I can watch Breakfast TV. While Lee is eating slowly (he has no energy even after a good night's sleep), I finish my food, go to the bathroom, get dressed, then start preparing lunch and our evening meal. I help Lee into the bathroom and dress him. This takes a good hour.

We then sit in the lounge and decide what needs to be done today, after opening and discussing our mail. I need to listen to my CD of Verdi's Requiem as Salisbury Musical Society (150) of which I am a member (second contralto), is going to Berlin for the Millennium to join forces with the Symphony Orchestra and Choirs and I have a rehearsal this evening in South Wiltshire Girls' Grammar School Hall.

At noon, we have a light lunch of freshly picked salad ingredients from our neighbours' allotment, with Wiltshire ham from Waitrose, our local supermarket. At 12.30 I leave home on my 18-gear mountain bike travelling the one and a half miles alongside the River Avon on the cycleway, to work. I park my bike on the roof of the Library, taking it up the three storeys in the lift.

I greet my colleagues, check the daily time-table to see who is in and on duty and to see what I am doing for the next four hours. I can concentrate on my job, serving the public, safe in the knowledge that our son, daughter-in-law and new baby grandson Jacob, will visit Grandad for an hour to see to his needs, the men talking of engineering, cars and house maintenance. My husband was Chief Designer at A E Goetze (formerly Wellworthy) which closed its Salisbury branch earlier this year.

Two colleagues go off for lunch and I check on ongoing tasks, read my e-mail, answer enquiries on the telephone and help any reader who approaches the desk for assistance. I set up the Reader/Printer for a gentleman who is researching the *Salisbury Journal* newspaper for the last hundred years for any printed/photographic information on his village, Pitton, about which he is compiling a parish study for the millennium. At least four times during the afternoon I will show readers Viewpoint Terminal where they can look up their own Library details, find out local information (clubs, societies), request a book and search the catalogue which shows every book in every Library in Wiltshire.

Four staff are on duty, so we start the ten minute tea break rota. At 17.00 hours I leave for home, the Department being manned for another two hours, and resume my home life.

I warm up the evening meal in the microwave oven and watch the 6 o'clock news on BBC TV. Then it's change of clothes and off to choir. Home again at 9.30pm, I talk to Lee for half an hour (quality time together) then prepare us for bed, falling asleep as soon as my head touches the pillow.

Pat Goodship

Memories of Compton Bassett extend back to childhood when, whilst a young teenager during each school summer holiday, walking from Cherhill by way of the public footpaths through woods was safe and enjoyable. This journey was made daily for the purpose of harvesting blackcurrants at Compton House, then owned by the Shepherd-Cross family who still live close by.

In 1975, married and with two small children, Briarleaze beckoned. Having lived in Calne for almost three years this was bliss and has remained so. How pleasant it is to sit in the garden and listen to the birds and the church bells.

The village is almost as it was then – a rural farming community with no street lights or mains gas supply – and although many of the villagers have changed the community atmosphere is still apparent.

The relatively close proximity of both the M4 motorway and mainline railway stations at Swindon and Chippenham have encouraged commuter growth in to the village. Increased property prices have meant that children who have entered adulthood have moved out of the village, but still have their roots within. The village shop has disappeared, but the public house remains. There is minimal public transport; most homes own at least one car.

The Village Flower Show, once a highlight of summer for avid gardeners and cooks, has ceased – probably caused by the acquisition of freezers, convenience foods and the change in gardening fashions; cultivation giving way to lawned gardens with trees and shrubs, patios and barbecues.

In the mid 1980's the White Horse (pub) tug of war team was renowned in the area. Training sessions on land above the village included large drums filled with concrete being hoisted up on a pulley over a gantry.

Compton Hall Amateur Dramatic Society (CHADS), formed in 1995, has become an integral part of the community. Village talent has been encouraged and nurtured by new blood. Twice-yearly productions ranging from variety to suspense have been performed for audiences who have been lucky enough to obtain tickets.

The Village Hall Management Committee has recently been able to rebuild the play area for the younger children after obtaining grants to the sum of £20,000. The hall is used regularly for dog training and other activities including church services whilst St. Swithin's Church was repaired.

The annual Church Fête is another memorable event for everyone, with children's painting competitions and skittles amongst the attractions. A hot air balloon flight is often the main prize in the raffle.

In 1977 – Queen Elizabeth II's Silver Jubilee – the village was a blaze of colour and excitement with wheelbarrow races, decorated gates and village party full of community spirit. May the arrival of 2000AD be as memorable.

Norman Gould

An eventual move to rural Wiltshire from the industrialised West Midlands was, although unsaid at the time, effectively part of my marriage vows. As the son of a factory worker at Massey Ferguson (a name not unknown in Wiltshire) married to the daughter of a Wiltshire bookmaker (a pastime not unknown in Coventry), we spent the majority of the last decade of the millennium living in Winterslow and Salisbury, before moving to Warminster in 1997.

Living in the centre of Warminster symbolises life in rural Wiltshire. The air is clean, the people are friendly and the shops sell all manner of goods that are not vacuum-sealed and can still be bought in prime number quantities. Tractors with laden trailers rumble through the Town Centre at all hours, the Council's summer hanging baskets are a joy to behold, and the *Warminster Journal* is a must for the Sutton Veny cricket reports alone. However, the Jewels in the Crown are the large, undulating and open fields that typify Wiltshire countryside. The contrasting colours of red poppies, yellow rape and blue flax in spring and summer are, indeed, an artist's paradise.

That said, life in Warminster is not all beer and skittles. We do not need a watch to know when it's closing time, alterations to the menus of the many local take-aways can be studied on the pavement at weekends, and my children are now familiar with a variety of phrases that would cause the examiners angst if used in GCSE English. Environmentally, the road outside our home seems to be dug up whenever Swindon Town concede a goal. It is also a mystery as to why the existence of the Warminster bypass still appears unknown to many HGV operators.

Nevertheless, there are few places that I would rather live. Nearby cities such as Salisbury and Bath offer a wider range of shops, more entertainment and better rail services. However, they are also symbolised by expensive housing, inadequate car parking and one-way systems that are about as useful as a crop circle is to a farmer! Although not exactly cosmopolitan, West Wiltshire (and Warminster in particular) is a wonderful place to live, work and visit. I am happy with my lot and am now proudly on my way to being an honorary Moonraker.

Pat Gould

Our cottage is in Ogbourne St George and so the Ridgeway Path is on our doorstep. Hikers and walkers often take the wrong turning and end up on our doorstep too. Festooned with maps and buckling under the weight of guide books they seem unaware that the path they seek is only a few yards away. I fervently hope that they never attempt a more exotic or far-flung expedition. But then why should they. I've lived in Wiltshire for twenty-four years and I love the patchwork folds of the rolling hills and fields where they fall away from the Ridgeway.

In the spring of 1999 the cottage was re-thatched. The old thatch had done us well for over twenty years but had become mossy, straggly and sagging. The thatchers arrived each day carrying two terrier dogs called Pip and Sam on the back of their lorry. The dogs' main function appeared to be to curl up in the bales of straw and sleep but I was assured that their real purpose was to catch and deter rats. The only time I ever saw them move, however, was when I proffered them slices of smoked ham from the fridge and discovered that I had suddenly acquired two canine friends for life – or at least until the roof was completed.

The thatchers were plied with trays of tea, coffee and biscuits and despite some days of foul weather worked on stoically in atrocious conditions to strip off the layers of old thatch and to prepare the new. The cottage became surrounded by vats of water-reed and bundles of sticks and spars and, as we approached the millennium, it somehow pleased me to see a traditional craft being plied all around us as the brand-new thatch took shape. It will hopefully last until at least 2020 – a defiant rural statement to offset the concrete, glass and steel of the twenty-first century.

It was hard to live in a cottage surrounded by scaffolding. Each window seemed like a prison cell as you looked out through the "bars" instead of onto fields, trees and the Ridgeway Path. But then at last all was finished and as the scaffolding was removed the cottage emerged like a butterfly folding over its swooping, bright straw wings. I marvelled at how all the different materials could be transformed into a neat, trimmed, patterned work of art and was pleased that walkers taking the wrong turn would have this to look on as they retraced their footsteps. Our own new millennium dome to see in the twenty-first century.

Ed Gosling, age 13

I have lived on a farm all of my life but I never get fed up with the big empty fields that surround my house. It is almost as if they are lying in wait ready to pounce and swallow it. The farm has many buildings that are arranged in a rectangle. In the middle there is a dirty grey courtyard. Some buildings are used for storing grain and some are used for keeping a small Guernsey herd in.

The house I live in has four bedrooms, the garden outside the house is full of roses, shrubs and unusual plants. Also there are usually four or five tennis, football and cricket balls lost in the garden. I have a half-size football goal in the back garden.

Life at the turn of the century   51

The farm has many scenes. My favourite scene is when the golden morning sun rises behind the woodland on the hill and then the brown and white cows turn golden as they eat the grass. All this takes place in the morning just half-a-mile away from my house.

In the summer and holidays I usually spend most of the day playing football and helping on the farm. In the morning I might help on the milk carton machine. This machine fills cartons up with milk. In the afternoon I usually help on bale cart or do the lawns. On bale cart I pick up the bales with a fork tractor and then load them on to the trailer. Every year my rate goes up by 50p. I am now on £2 for I started at ten years old.

Twenty years ago the small farm industry was doing well because of high cattle and wheat prices. The farmers then were rich. Now all the small farms are going out of business because of more imports and so the price of cows and wheat has fallen. I fear soon ours will as well. In the future I fear that people won't bother with farming anymore and so they will sell their land for housing.

Jennifer Greatwood, age 15

I think that my life in Wiltshire is pretty ordinary. At the moment I am in Year 10 and I am revising for my end-of-year exams. I will be taking these exams at the end of June. After it is the summer and then Year 11.

Apart from school there are some other activities which take up a lot of my time. One of these activities is music. Now I am in the school band brass ensemble, choir, the Trowbridge and District Youth Band (TDYB) and until July I am in the school production of "Me and My Girl". I enjoy all of the music-based activities I take part in, although they take up a lot of time. Being in the different groups gives me the chance to become a better player and broaden the varieties of music I play. Also being in these groups I have made many new friends. Being in these groups I have played in some different locations. Some of these have been formal and others have not been as formal. The most recent events I have played at are a school fête and the music teachers parents' evening. Taking part in the functions has built up my confidence.

I am enjoying being in the production because it is good fun but hard work. There are lots of rehearsals which are hard and sometimes a little bit tedious. Being in the production is good because I enjoy singing and performing. I also feel it is good because I am taking part in an extra-curricular activity and I will have something to show and be proud of when it is finished.

Another one of the activities I take part in outside school is having a Saturday job. I work as a waitress at a pub near where I live. I will have been working there a year at the end of July. I enjoy working because I get to meet people and I have learnt some skills. At work I have to: lay the tables; wash up; prepare plate combinations; sort cutlery; serve food; clear away. The job has helped me to be more confident. I enjoy work because I am earning money and I don't have to rely on my parents as much. Working has also helped me get an idea of what working is like and how it might be similar when I am grown-up.

Roy Gregory

Ten-to-nine. Ducks have been fed, only two eggs today. But what a picking of raspberries and strawberries this morning, the June sunshine has come exactly right after the spring rain. Too bad it's Monday again, back to work.

Pull off the drive. Will there be roadworks in Westbury today? They seem to spring up without warning, always bring a moan but rarely do they add more than a couple of minutes to my journey. No, it's a clear run through, but anyway I have to get petrol. My usual, fourteen pounds worth, that will last a week or so, although I see it has gone up by a penny a litre.

On out of Westbury, the Bratton Road. How I love this drive, five days a week and I never tire of it. Today is a gem, the velvet green of Bratton Castle and the all-seeing eye of the White Horse, watching with the slanting sun and me over a sea of blue linseed to Roundway Down and the Alton Barnes horse beyond. Even the cement works is a different hue, a new blend of light and shade every day, every hour indeed.

At Bratton there's plenty of life. Children have been safely delivered to school. The lollipop lady helps the last of the returning Mums over the road, with their straggle of two- and three-year-olds. Pensioners emerge from the post office with the day's paper. It's then I get behind the bus and I know I will have to follow it to Erlestoke. If I hadn't needed petrol... No matter, you can't drive this road much faster than a bus anyway.

A line of cars builds up behind the bus, four, five of us, one to a car. It always seems ironic, this procession of vehicles behind one which could carry all of us. I can see two passengers on the bus, which proudly announces on its rear (above the advertisement for Volkswagens) a capacity for thirty-nine. I could take the bus to work, but the last bus back to Westbury is far too early to return on. Would I actually choose public transport anyway? Even my old car has creature comforts (well, a medium wave radio and a heater), and its just where I want it, when I want it. A bus ride today would be fine, but who wants to wait at bus-stops in February?

Journey completed, Erlestoke Prison. I pull into the driveway, look at my watch, twenty minutes from Dilton Marsh as usual. "It's Roy. Come to do the evening shift?" The gate-house gags, never original, form a welcoming gauntlet. And so, another day, in the incongruous Wiltshire countryside, seeing prisoners about all manner of life's problems, between meetings about how, one day, we might supposedly do it all more efficiently.

Journey home. That perfect, privileged, unwinding drive. Home. Ducks to feed, raspberries to pick.

In my garden there are hollyhocks, cornflowers, roses, lavender, nasturtiums, lemon balm, pumpkins and an elder tree. In summer, we make champagne from its flowers; in autumn, wine from its berries.

This garden, bursting with life and colour, is the territory of five treasured cats who are constantly at my side as I hunt for strawberries or pick chickweed leaves for eczema ointment. If I am still here when I am old and grey, little children will dare each other to run past my gate, scared of the funny old woman who wanders through her garden talking to her cats.

There are two rows of terraced houses here, in a quiet backwater in the centre of Trowbridge. The terraces face each other, separated by long narrow gardens and leafy, traffic-free lanes. The houses were built approximately 150 years ago as homes for workers in the woollen industry. Today, they are Grade II listed to protect their unusual layout.

On summer evenings, hot air balloons from Bath float over the chimney pots and children play in the lanes. Cats curl up on shed roofs and Dasher the dog who lives opposite makes yet another attempt at freedom by escaping over the garden fence.

Many friends of mine hardly know their neighbours but here there is a true community spirit. Someone is always willing to help find Dasher or unblock a drain.

At both ends of the street onto which the lanes run are two corner shops. One is owned by an Indian family selling everything from chapati flour to baked beans. The other is Rose's Bakery with cat biscuits in dustbins and faded birthday cards and a bell over the door announcing each arrival and departure. Nightshift workers returning from the factories in the early hours of the morning are treated to a delicious smell of fresh bread baking as they pass by.

Opposite Rose's is a house with a FOR SALE sign staked in the gravel. Until the beginning of this year, this belonged to a man called Paul. On summer afternoons he would drag an armchair onto the front porch and fall asleep behind his paper while his ancient transistor radio blasted out military marching music. He decorated his front garden with orange traffic cones, children's foil windmills and grew plants in a shopping trolley. In his back garden, he rigged up an ingenious display of bird scarers to stop the pigeons from eating the seeds he planted religiously every Spring. These included Tesco's carrier bags, plastic bottles and tin foil pie dishes speared on poles. That nothing ever did grow was more to do with the crazy tilt of his soil than the pilfering bird population, but the care he gave to his garden was genuine, if not conventional.

Early in 1999, Paul died, the traffic cones and windmills were removed from his front garden and a FOR SALE sign went up in their place. But on July afternoons, you could almost swear you can still hear the sound of marching music playing in a magical garden.

Vashti Hallissey, age 15

My name is Vashti Hallissey, I have two sisters and one brother and I have lived in Trowbridge for the past eleven and a half years. I live in a Victorian house called 'Penrhyn' which I adore. Two fantastic things about it are the huge wild garden and flat roof. From there I can see the whole of Trowbridge and the hills in the distance. I love to tip-toe up there at night, alone, and gaze at the spell-binding stars and radiant lights of the sleeping town. 'Penrhyn' is a house of character and many of my own most joyous times have been spent there.

At the moment I attend John of Gaunt Secondary School which, on the whole, I enjoy. Sometimes I think about how devastating it will be to leave behind all the people and places that I've seen almost every day for a large part of my life. However, on the bright side, it will be like kissing goodbye to my childhood and becoming independent and liberated in one day. It is like the unlocking of a cage and a release into the unknown.

I am fond of Wiltshire but I crave change, Trowbridge has been a safe, tranquil, friendly place to grow up in but in the twenty-first century I want to live somewhere fascinating, constantly changing and dynamic. Where ideas and inspiration flourish surrounded by harsh dark walls that jut out into the silver clouds and slice into the cobalt sky. Somewhere that I can truly live and progress, meet incredible people and feel the fire and energy of the city.

However, Wiltshire will always be a place that I will return to throughout my life. It is a link to a person I used to be and a life that I used to lead. I feel welcome and content here, no place in the world gives me the same feeling of warmth and acceptance, a place where I belong. No matter what dramatic and awesome events take place in the twenty-first century some things never change, and Wiltshire, my beloved home, is one of them.

Stephen Hardy, age 10

My parents are divorced so I kind of live in two houses. I mostly live with my mum. I am sometimes picked up after school by my dad and sleep over the weekend. When my birthday comes I feel like I have two — one at my mum's and another one at dad's. My mum lives in Winterslow and my father lives in Coombe Bissett.

My father is a policeman and my mum works at Porton army base.

I have two step-sisters and three step-brothers. When I am with mum and my step-dad, we like to watch car racing at Thruxton and Donnington. Sometimes we watch bike racing, my step-dad likes motorbikes.

I go to school in Winterslow, before I went to school in Coombe Bissett. I went to my first playgroup in Swindon, then I moved house to Wilton.

When I have some spare time I play on my computer. When I am with my dad he sometimes plays squash and I enjoy playing as well.

My ambition, when I am older, is to be a marine biologist because my family used to go camping by the sea when we had a caravan and a boat. I first had the ambition when I went to a sea life centre and first watched a video on sharks, so I bought a book on sea life and thought about making my own folder. Because I want to do this I will most likely have to go to college or university to get a degree but I don't mind.

Life in Wiltshire has its good and bad sides because where I live does not have any entertainment such as a cinema or bowling alley. When we get older and want to go out to shops our mums and dads have to take us to the places we want to go such as Trowbridge and Bath. The other alternative is to catch a train or bus, these do not however run very frequently. The trains are not very reliable as they do not always come on time or sometimes the stops are limited which means that the train does not always stop at the smaller local stations.

The good sides are that we have lots of fields surrounding the village where you can go on long walks and see wildlife in its natural home. We have a manor house and a park to play in which is set in a pretty area with trees surrounding it. There is a local village shop which is run by Harry and Marion Thorn who are very nice people, they make sure that a wide range of goods are on sale and it is used regularly by the villagers. Nearly all of my friends come from the village and I have met most of them at my local school. The school is quite small in numbers compared to others in the area, my teacher at the moment is Mrs Backhouse who is also the Head teacher.

In Westwood there is a social club which is owned by the members. The club holds lots of different functions like parties, skittles, discos, jumble sales and lots of other things.

The towns surrounding Westwood are Bradford on Avon and Trowbridge. We can also walk to even smaller places like Iford where you can visit the manor house and gardens and Avoncliffe where there is a canal and an aqueduct.

Living in Westwood is excellent because every morning I wake up to fresh air and the sound of birds singing in the trees; people also have time to say good morning to you. If you lived in the centre of a big town or city you would wake up to the smell of car fumes and people bustling along the streets on their way to work.

In Compton Chamberlain we are mainly affluent with a number of young children. The only teenagers in the village come from an old established farming family and are away at boarding school. The greatest proportion is of home owners with only about nine homes tied to agriculture, estate or domestic work.

Thirteen years ago, when I came, there were four working farms, a motor mechanic, newsagent and roofing contractor all running their businesses from their own houses, a gamekeeper, a waterkeeper, a Post Office-cum-shop, and a postman living in the village. Today the Park house and the Dower House still have their staff, including the newsagent, game- and waterkeepers, but the number of farms is down to two. The motor mechanic has retired and the Post Office has long gone. The roofing contractor has gone from strength to strength, and an architect who works from home has arrived, but in general employment is more than ever outside the village.

We focus for shopping on Salisbury, though some stubborn souls try to avoid it by shopping in Dinton, Fovant or Wilton. Getting there is the problem, and carrying the stuff back. Most refuse to consider anything except a car as being practical. We used also to have the mobile library visit the village, but only during the week which meant those away at work couldn't use it, needing a trip away anyway. So it fell into disuse and was cancelled. When you get so old you can no longer drive, move out.

Fortunately most people who live here see politics as a necessary evil; no one really wants to do it. We're too small for a Parish Council and hold Parish Meetings twice a year. Even then finding the three representatives of Chairman, Treasurer and Secretary is hard enough.

If you want a picture of political colour, it's hard to judge since people keep their views close to their chests. But it's probably reluctant Conservative in the main; reluctant in that they don't like the changes that occurred after Mrs Thatcher left all those years ago. We continually vote in an Independent District Councillor, which I think we all find a relief, because it allows us to be apolitical, which is very important in such a small community.

We have a regular bridge club on alternate Fridays, to which several villagers go. We have a bellringing practice once a week on Thursday evening though the number of ringers living in the village is now not enough for the six fine bells in the church. We rely on ringers from Dinton and Salisbury joining us, for us to be able to ring for the service every fortnight. There is a vibrant cricket club but so few villagers are involved as players that it is almost a lodger in our midst. Many villagers support it by fundraising and all welcome the club, though we don't see the players as often as we used to. They used to have to drag all the way up the village street to the village hall for the teas, and the sound of their studded boots brought people out to welcome them as they went by. Some of the gents of the village play golf together, and there are three aeroplane pilots from different families in the village who fly together on occasion. This has come about from the defence connection of this region.

We were all upset a couple of years ago to find we were continually being pestered by Jehovah's Witnesses; even on Easter Day itself. None of us here subscribe to that denomination. In general there aren't many churchgoers at all in the village. Most who go attend the local Anglican church which is at the old heart of the village, though not all who do were baptised Anglican. There are a couple of Roman Catholics who regularly go to Mass in Tisbury or Wardour, with the old, thriving Roman Catholic community there.

We have a village notice board. For about eight years there was a locally produced news-sheet called the *Compton Courier*, which I took my turn at editing for about two years. Now we rely on a section reserved for our village in the *Three Towers* which is a community magazine produced in Fovant for Fovant, Sutton Mandeville and Compton Chamberlayne.

Mrs. L. Mae Harry

My husband and I retired to West Wiltshire in 1982, after working in Bristol, where we were born. We bought a bungalow in a quiet lane on a hill in Crockerton, surrounded by trees and fields. There is greenery everywhere, and flowers in their season. My neighbours are hidden from me by their trees and hedges, but we can rely on each other when need arises.

My life is easy now, compared to thirty-six years in Bristol Telephone Exchange. I love my garden, which is fairly small and surrounds the house, and have watched the shrubs we planted grow to maturity. Living with plants makes me very aware of the changing seasons.

We had two Labradors when we moved here, and after their passing I acquired a whippet cross bitch. Our daily walk is usually in the vicinity of Lake Shearwater and the surrounding woods, part of Longleat Estate, where we meet fellow dog-walkers. We watch the rise and fall of the waters, the fishermen, the sailing boats and the ducks and herons.

I shop twice a week in Warminster, which I reach by car. There is a bus once a day, but I would find it hard to carry heavy bags up the hill. I think Warminster is just the right size, with sufficient shops for my needs, and the bonus of free parking. The centre of the town is busy, though with less heavy vehicles since the bypass opened. I can usually expect to greet an acquaintance when I shop, especially on Fridays which is W.I. Market day.

These acquaintances are linked to my other leisure activity, the Women's Institute. I joined Warminster Institute in 1983 to make friends and have the opportunity to further my interest in knitting and embroidery. After my husband died in 1988 I was elected to the committee, and have been President for over six years now. This has brought me many friendships. I enjoy the planning, and occasionally write stories and sketches to amuse the members.

We try to give something back to the community, and support the Summer Hospital Fête by running a Grocery Tombola, which raises a useful sum. Some of us tend the flowers in the Hospital. We also

---

contribute to the Beckford Day Centre each year – by holding a Jumbo Bring-and-Buy sale. We know we may need these facilities one day. I attended the Fracture Clinic when I broke my wrist.

So, apart from W.I., my days are filled with tending my garden, including the hedges and grass, reading *The Times* and library books, and walking with the dog. I watch television or listen to music while knitting or sewing. I have a video recorder, but no computer or mobile phone: I don't need them. I cook a hot meal daily, have a low-fat, high-fibre diet and am basically healthy. Living in Wiltshire suits me fine.

Paul Hayward, age 9

We live in a close village community. Everyone knows everyone and we have a village school, hall, shop, bakery, post office, recreation ground and two churches.

I arrive at school at 8.45 am with my mum. We come by car because we live on the outskirts of the village. We have different lessons each day, we have first play at 10.30 am and second play and lunch at 12.00. We then have more lessons and go home at 3.10 pm.

There are no leisure centres in Landford, only the recreation ground. So I go to Salisbury for swimming club, the only leisure activity I do in Landford is run by our chapel, called Shell Club, where we do snooker, table tennis and hockey.

My hobbies are football and cricket and swimming, also I like watching all the different kinds of birds that we get on our farm.

We live on a market garden which means that we are very busy as a family. I like to help with the work. In the school holiday I get some money for helping, to spend on my holidays.

We get up early each morning and are sometimes late to bed, when I go delivering to the market with my dad. I have two older brothers, a cat, dog, fish and a donkey. I like looking after my animals.

Friends: I have a lot of friends at school but because we live out of the main village, I tend to play with my cousins who live next door to us. We do lots of things: we play football, cricket we also go fishing down my dad's lake.

Charlie Hey, age 10

My name is Charlie Hey and I am 10 years-old (nearly 11). I was born in Queen Charlotte's Hospital in London on the 14th of July. This is Bastille Day in France, when the French overthrew their King, whose name was Louis. One of my other names is Louis!

I moved to Bradford on Avon with my new baby brother Jack and my Mother and Father when I was two years old. It was a lovely change from London just like living in a very large park.

We moved to a Victorian house that used to be a coach house (there are still some of the original cobbles underneath the floorboards) to the big house next door named Gramby House. This house was burnt down in 1913 by the suffragettes because an M.P. was staying there who didn't want women to get the vote. It was rebuilt as two separate dwellings.

We don't live too near the road and are opposite a vineyard. On the other side of our house there are miles of peaceful fields to walk in. We have a big garden so we have lots of animals which I love. We have eight chickens, the rooster is called Oxo and the two main hens are Sage and Onion. We have six cats all named after sweets. The mother cat is called Wine Gum and her babies have names like Toffee, Bugsy (Humbug) Dime, Kit-Kat and Penguin. We also have one rabbit, two fish and Kramer the cockatiel, named by my Dad after a character in 'Seinfeld' whose hair looks like a cockatiel's crest.

I go to Westwood with Iford School and have lots of good friends. I am in Class 4 and will be leaving school at the end of term.

My hobbies are football, Warhammer, Athletics, playing on the playstation and on the P.C. and drawing.

My Dad (Stan Hey) writes books and is a journalist on the *Independent* on Sunday. My mum (Wendy Hey) does painting and teaches Yoga.

I love living here because it is very quiet and peaceful with no pollution. I enjoy Bradford Swimming Pool, the library, the video shop and like going to the Dandy Lion pub every Sunday. I enjoy walking in the Tithe Barn and am amazed how old it is. When I grow up I would like to be an archaeologist.

Felicity Hill, age 10

My name is Felicity Hill I live in Dauntsey. Dauntsey is in the north-west of Wiltshire. I go to Brinkworth Earl Danbys Primary School but I am soon going to secondary school. I have lived in Dauntsey all my life and I like where I live. Dauntsey is near Malmesbury and my brother goes to the school there. We do our shopping in Safeways by scanning in our food with hand-held scanners, and then paying for it. In our class at school we have 35 children so it is a bit of a squash. My best friend is Josie and we have been friends for two years now. I have about twenty stick insects for pets and they are about 10cms long.

On Tuesdays I go to Guides with some of my friends. It is fun, but if we don't find a leader soon Guides will stop. Sometimes on Monday I go riding. I usually ride a pony called Beau he is very well behaved. At playtime Jo and I play skipping, or all of my friends play together. I also enjoy reading, some of my favourites are the Narnia books, *Gobbolino the Witch's Cat* and the Annual Ark books.

At Christmas the most popular present was a furby. Furbies are electronic pets and they are good fun. I have one called Toylo and he plays games, talks and eats. My favourite food is sausage and chips with vinegar (yum!) I collect Wade figures and beany babies. I have 25 beany babies and I also have three bears and seven teeny bean babies. The Wade is worth £300 but I am not going to sell it. I won £100 in a drawing competition and it was the best competition I have ever won.

The Village where I live is a Person: The village where I live is very tall. Its head is high on the chalk downland close to Win Green, the highest point in Wiltshire, while its feet are planted firmly in the heavy clay and lush water-meadows of the River Don. The A30 road bisects it like a slender belt around its ample belly.

The skeleton of the village is made up of five farms, two of which have been in the same family for centuries, while the others have been passed down over at least two or three generations. The highest farm is mainly arable and in summer the head of the village has a thick mane of undulating wheat and barley, while in the winter it shivers under a severe crew-cut. The lower farms all have dairies and varying numbers of sheep; so in the spring the air is full of the sound of lambs and an early morning walk is sometimes enhanced by the sight of a new calf, born during the night and still very unsteady on its spindly legs.

The soft tissues of the village are made up of people like my friends and I, with large gardens or a few acres of land on which we have either assorted poultry, a small flock of sheep, a couple of horses or an organic vegetable garden. Mainly self-employed or professional people, our occupations include builder, engineer, teacher, doctor, dentist and vet. We tend to regard our animals as part of our families, keeping them with us and tending to their needs long after they have ceased to be productive and trying to ensure that they have a painless and dignified death when the time finally comes. We share our implements and our skills to the benefit of all. One person can shear sheep and one kill and draw poultry; another has a tractor and topper and is much in demand in summer, while his neighbour, who is highly skilled with a chain saw, provides logs for our woodburners.

The skin of our village is that which most people see, the thatched cottages, old stone mansions, modern stone bungalows and brick council houses many with colourful and productive gardens tended by the interesting and varied collection of people who live here. Many are retired and have plenty of time to work on their houses and gardens, while others are trying to run a business and bring up a family and just about manage to cut the grass at the weekend.

What you will not see as you pass through the village is its soul, the spirit of community and the high level of caring for friends and neighbours which binds the village together and makes Donhead St. Andrew the best place in the world to live.

Annette Hitch

I wonder if a job like mine will be necessary in a hundred years from now? I am employed by the Local Education Authority to help deaf children in this rural county of Wiltshire. The work is itinerant and travelling across rolling downland and through leafy lanes is one of its joys.

There are, however, certain difficulties working in a rural county. A lot of my time is spent travelling; when I first began working for Wiltshire, ten years ago, our office was in Salisbury, an hour and a half drive from the north of the county. We now have a second office in Trowbridge. Parents also have problems attending support meetings because of the travelling time involved. Services are very different in urban areas. There staff often specialise with particular age groups; in Wiltshire we are organised geographically. Wiltshire has no School for the Deaf. The few children requiring this provision go to schools in other counties. Government policy currently is to include children with special needs in their local mainstream schools. By necessity and parental choice the majority of Wiltshire's deaf children do this already!

I have the privilege of working with families, guiding parents through the mysteries of hearing aids and language development. Deafness can be detected very early, with some babies being diagnosed at four days old. The job has its controversies and the centuries-old debate, whether a deaf child should sign or speak, still rages.

When the deaf or partially hearing child starts school I go too. Explaining the implications of hearing impairment to the child's teacher and support assistant is one of my key tasks. I also talk to the child's classmates, playing tapes of what it's like to be deaf and letting them listen through hearing and radio aids. I get to know many of the children really well; some I teach regularly and, theoretically, I could contribute to a child's education from a few months old to the age of eighteen.

It's brilliant to be able to celebrate the successes of many of these young people. Sam, who is at university, has set up a support group for other deaf students; Richard, still at school, is providing counselling for pupils with problems and Chris is a talented musician!

About half the causes of deafness can be attributed to genetic factors. The medical profession is gradually beginning to identify the defective genes. Maybe this information will eventually allow prospective parents to make informed choices. This research is very much in its infancy and the ethical dilemmas are huge. New vaccines are being marketed all the time; deafness caused by rubella, mumps and measles has been virtually eradicated, and before long, I am sure there will be an immunisation for all strains of meningitis.

Will a job like mine still exist in a hundred years from now? There are likely to be far fewer deaf children and education will be radically different, so, I suspect not.

Jean Hopkins

The garden's getting too much for us! As I sit here in the sun, a bag of frozen peas on my back ("Ten minutes," the osteopath had said, "then ten minutes with a hot water bottle"), I can see edges that need trimming and weeds that should be pulled. But I cannot bear the thought of moving, I love both garden and village. We enjoy the neighbours and dear dogs who pass through the kissing gate and under the chestnut trees, the children who run down after a day at school to talk to the horses, the pensioner who jauntily walks eight miles every day. "Bit better this morning," he cheerfully calls through sun, wind, rain or snow.

People are what make village life and we also know so many through the various organisations, the Church with its band of volunteers – Sunday

School teachers, Choir, altar flower arrangers, cleaners, bell ringers, and the grass cutter who, for pocket money, has mowed the churchyard for almost forty long years. Now there is talk of floodlighting for the millennium. Can we raise the money for this, I wonder? It never ceases to amaze me how we do.

This year's Church Fête raised hundreds of pounds in just three hours. In a huge hat, Debbie from the shop opened the event. Schoolchildren danced round the maypole, their proud parents looking on; there was tense rivalry for the tug-o-war between teams representing The Volunteer Inn and the shop, girlfriends and wives anxiously cheering from the sidelines as they strained the long rope. Later a roar of delight as, from behind a sheet painted with hairy chests, the Tower Captain of the Bellringers emerged as winner of the Knobbly Knees Competition!

Cakes and Produce stalls were sold out within the hour so their holders could wander round the White Elephant, books, toys or garden stalls, partake of ice-cream, hot dogs or alcoholic drinks (licence granted by the Court). For children a bouncy castle, lucky dip or face painting.

Young children are well catered for in the village – there are Mums and Toddlers, Pre-School, Infants and Junior School, then Rainbows, Brownies and Guides. Ladies have a sewing group, 'Coffee Pots' or 'Over 60's', the latter also welcome men. These are just a few of the events and people who touch our lives at some time during the year. We are included and warmed by this large village family. Old and young, rich or poor, mix together. The man who lays the hedges is as respected as the magistrate, and the barrister as much a friend as the builder who greets you in a rich Wiltshire voice, rounded, earthy and solid as the lovely Lyneham Bank that looks down on us folk in the Dauntsey Vale.

How could I possibly leave all this?

In fact that hot water bottle's done a lot of good... I think... if I'm careful, I might just manage to dead-head those roses.

● ●

I've lived in Wiltshire all my life and although I know no different, I love it. I live on a farm in the hamlet of Beckhampton, just off the A4. My house is called Galteemoe and is named after a famous racehorse. My Great-Grandfather bought the farm and house from Sam Darling, the racehorse trainer, in Beckhampton in 1922. Since then it has been passed down through our family. Our house is approximately 400 years old.

We farmed cattle until the BSE crisis in 1996 when we suffered greatly due to poor demands for beef. We used to farm 200 cows, we now only farm 40. We are mainly an arable farm so the summer months are hard work. This means our family do not see each other much.

We employ two men to help us throughout the year. Belonging to a farming family is a lot of hard work. However, having 1400 acres of land has lots of bonuses: it means I can ride my pony over the fields whenever I like.

We live one mile from Avebury which is a World Heritage site. So unfortunately this attracts a lot of tourists. I can also ride up to the West Kennet Long Barrow because we farm the land around that area.

A great thing about Wiltshire is the friendliness and laid-back approach of everyone. One of my favourite things about living in Wiltshire is that hardly anything has changed in the last 50-100 years. Only three or four houses have been built. Beckhampton is very small with few modern houses. The gardens nearly all have lots of garden space full of pretty flowers.

Beckhampton is very close to Avebury school which is an excellent school with small classes and brilliant sports and music facilities.

Lots of families go on holiday during the year whether it is to Blackpool or Austria and Wiltshire provides an excellent contrast to this. At Christmas I went to London and I realised how polite and how they never looked happy or said please or thank-you. I realised how lucky I am to live in Wiltshire at the end of the second millennium. I just hope this remains the case for the future generations.

Gwyneth Jackson

A wispy cloud races across a clear blue July sky as a busy breeze rustles through the ash tree's leaves. It creates dancing dappled shadows which pattern the lawn and the many-paged, numerous-sectioned, Sunday newspaper, which informs its reader, grappling with its unwieldy pages, of the current world catastrophes and the unsavoury activities of some of its famous citizens.

Occasionally there is a stronger gust of wind, as if it's saying, "I'm being gentle now but don't forget my strength, for I'm a Wiltshire wind and I rarely sleep. I sweep the downlands and swirl through the towns and villages. I lift the snow from the ploughed fields and dump it in the lanes. I break and uproot trees, snap power lines and gleefully seek out newly erected fences and traffic cones. I create crop circles in fields of ripening grain without the help of extraterrestrial forces or folk dragging logs. This year I've rippled over acre upon acre of linseed, its fragile blue flowers reflecting today's sky. Why so much this year? A European Union subsidy perhaps? I lift the hang-gliders off the downs and raise kites and then let them plunge into the 'so good for the butterflies' patches of nettles. When I snooze, gliders climb high on the thermals and giant, coloured hot air balloons drift across the sky."

Now the breeze slumbers and in the flower-perfumed air other sounds become clearer. The sound of children's voices as they race along the lane with their pet dogs, after spending part of the afternoon splashing in the village school's swimming pool. The drone of Sunday afternoon traffic along the bypass, the construction of which liberated our village seven years ago. The quarrelsome whine of a distant lawn mower, the rumble of a tractor, the click of a golf ball being hit and the whistle and chirps of many songbirds. The parent birds now taking a well-earned rest but they must still remain vigilant for a buzzard has recently set up home locally. Neither the birds, grey squirrels, wild rabbits or the neighbour's cat seem to mind the tuneless bleep of the mole deterrent, unfortunately neither does the mole.

A small plane circles overhead. We wonder if we or the spire of St.

Martin's Church, Zeals are the turning point for flying lessons from Compton Abbas and if they really have to cut out their engines here? They are, however, preferable to the juddering helicopters or, worse still, the fighter jets which leave us quivering and exclaiming, "My that was low," or something a little stronger.

A car roars down the lane, a mixture of engine noise and music, followed by a squeal of brakes. Did the driver really not expect anyone else to be about on this sunny afternoon in this corner of Wiltshire where it meets Dorset and Somerset?

Madeleine Jackson

In order to understand my view of life in Wiltshire there are some key facts that need to be explained. Firstly, I have only been living in the county since December 1998, so it is still a very new experience for me. Secondly, prior to this, I had spent my entire life both living and working in inner-London (where, indeed, I was born), so the changes in lifestyle have been profound and not a little dramatic.

Living in Wilsford we are between villages – Amesbury, with its high street shops and post office on one side of us, and the Woodfords, three linked villages with their church school, and an excellent pub on the river. When we first moved in our local vicar came to visit and we spent a pleasant time discussing a wide range of issues (over tea, of course), far more concerned with education and standards of living, than any specific religious message. We also visited our neighbours, where we seemed to be introduced to the entire village. Since all the people in Wilsford seem to have lived here for most of their lives, I am well aware that my partner and I will be 'the new ones' for quite some time to come.

When I get up in the morning, it is usually to the sound of the horses outside, fresh from the gallop at the back of our house. We are delighted to have woodpeckers, pheasants and other birds roaming around our garden and watching them usually delays my start to the day. Any work that I do is usually from home. I have my own 'office' with computer, fax and email, which connects me around the world, if necessary. However, at the end of the day, more often than not it is my sister and I who communicate our thoughts, highs and lows, as we summarise the day via email.

The bus service here is good but still rather limited, so we need to take the car on our shopping trips, either into Amesbury or, rather more frequently, to Salisbury. Salisbury is a delight with its contrasting collection of small, antiquated shops, supermarkets, plus an excellent market, selling local produce twice a week.

I love the fact that everyone here is so friendly. We have regular chats with our postwoman (when we are up in time for the early morning delivery) and even sent her a postcard from our recent holiday.

Due to the short time we have been here, our friends are still mostly from London, or its suburbs, but we are gradually building up our local friends. We love having people here, especially now that it's summer and we can eat our meals in the garden and, in the evening, watch the sun set. Because of our location, our visitors invariably stay overnight, if not longer, and seem to settle in to the point that we wonder if they are ever going to be on their way.

Recently, I undertook a work project that necessitated my visiting London once a week. The best part for me was, at the end of the day, catching the train home back to my beloved Wiltshire.

Sian James, age 15

What life? I ask myself. I never thought it possible to live in Wiltshire and still have a life, especially if like myself you are a member of the teenage society but perhaps I shouldn't be so negative.

The more I consider the conduct of Sian James throughout her life in Wiltshire, I actually realize I'm a fairly active person. Besides school and sleeping which my life hugely revolves around, I enjoy taking part in extra-curricular activities.

I am a member of the Trowbridge Town Youth Council: I felt it necessary to join because teenagers are screaming to be heard, yet coffin dodgers accuse us of being noisy or refuse to listen to our 'Whimpering', so I become their voice.

I may not possess the power or skill to solve world issues but I can represent the teenagers' community, we are residents of Wiltshire and deserve the right to be heard.

I don't just have a life in Wiltshire, I have other roles. One of them as a youth member is to be active and productive, to prove to old age pensioners that not all teenagers are juvenile delinquents, but are capable of acting like human beings: In fact my life in Wiltshire, especially compared to other districts, isn't really all that bad.

Mrs. H.A. Jemson

"Oh, you live in Stert – aren't you lucky, so pretty, and the view... "

"Stert, I'm afraid I've never heard of it, where is it?"

These are the two most common remarks I hear when people ask me where I live, but they are not surprising because my village is both very attractive and very hidden. Stert lies about two miles east of Devizes, tucked away on a south-facing slope, half concealed from the main road, looking across the Vale of Pewsey towards the northern edge of Salisbury Plain, with Etchilhampton Hill sheltering it from the north.

The view from the village is stunning, especially on a fine clear day when we can see down towards the Somerset border beyond Westbury and over to Upavon in the east. I live with my husband David in a cottage which was built, like several others hereabouts, around AD1600. The cottages are timber, wattle and daub construction, and many still thatched. Our cottage isn't thatched any longer but our huge barn, which is a Listed Building, is. We came to Stert in 1962, not long after we found jobs locally, and have been here longer than any other villagers except for Frank and Shirley Edwards, our neighbours at the farm next door.

Stert in the 1960s was still a small hamlet and most of the people were connected with farming or Devizes businesses. Now, like so many other places, it has had several new houses built and has grown into a commuting dormitory or place to which people retire.

Many years ago Stert had a school, a shop, a non-conformist chapel, a police house, a C of E church and a scattering of small farms. Today, just one large farm and the church remain. However, the church is well supported and organises community activities such as the August Pig Roast, and jollifications after Harvest Festival and the Carol Service.

For the Millennium Stert has decided to produce a village book and we are trying to contribute something about the history of our houses and various aspects of the village. This has entailed a good deal of toing and froing to New College, Oxford where much archive material is stored. This is because the college used to own a lot of the land and several of the cottages here, from about AD1300 to the mid-1960s. In fact we bought our cottage from New College in 1967, and called it Manor Cottage as it is next door to Manor Farm.

Now that David and I are retired we are sometimes asked, "What do you do to keep yourselves busy?" We usually say, "Oh, we go to parties in the village," which is true. But we also busy ourselves with gardening or doing something for the church (David has been a churchwarden for 28 years) or fishing or visiting our family or having grandchildren to stay or (most important) walking our Labrador... and so it goes on.

And for wider interest there are good things going on in Devizes – Art Exhibitions and concerts and the Summer Festival and Craft Fairs and charity 'dos', whilst organisations like the Women's Institute flourish in our next door village of Urchfont.

But of course all this does create a lot of traffic and some of us are beginning to feel we should make fewer journeys and lessen the noise and pollution. We do have bicycles but I'm afraid we don't use them as much as we should.

I think most people would regard Stert as a pleasant village to live in with good walks and an easy community whilst being close enough to a town supplying the everyday needs.

Miss E Jessop

● ●

The telephone rang. I was offered a job as a nanny in Chippenham, Wiltshire.

I have never been away from home. This was going to be the biggest decision of my life and only I could make it. I had a number of questions going through my head; could I cope with only seeing my family and close friends once a month. I was really unaware of what to expect, entering the grown-up world after living my life as a shy young girl, lacking confidence. Half of me wanted to pack my bags and leave without a second thought, whereas the other part of me was saying stay. I guess you could say I was torn between two lifestyles, not knowing which would be the best for me. I finally decided that I had to take the biggest step in my life.

Moving to Chippenham has been quite an eye-opener. It is so much different than the quiet village life I was used to. I consider myself to live in a friendly community which has a local mini-store, garage, bed and breakfast accommodation and several pubs. Behind my house is the main railway line. We also have Chippenham Community Hospital and Rowden Surgery nearby. There are several parks around for the children to play at, some offering more potential than others. The town centre is only a fifteen-minute walk away and it offers many facilities, considering the elderly, disabled and people with pushchairs.

As I am a nanny, I spend my working day carrying out activities with the children. This includes creative play and social skill development. This allows them to fulfil their needs and prepare them for when they start school. We enjoy visiting the Olympiad Leisure Centre in town, where we attend junior gymnastics, swimming and Toddler Blitz. On sunny days we like to have picnics in the park, feed the ducks and swans along the banks of the River Avon

Once the children's parents have come home from work I am off-duty. I really enjoy the company of the family. They treat me as one of them, not just somebody that works and lives in their home. I think this has also helped me to stay up here, for as long as I have.

I have made new friends up here now and we enjoy going out clubbing. We also enjoy going to the cinema and of course we enjoy going shopping in Bath. We have joined the Angel Leisure Club, which is always a great evening out.

Looking back now, the past year has been the best for me. I have learnt to accept me for being me. I've gained so much confidence and am now beginning to believe in myself and appreciate my abilities.

Not only do I thank myself and the people who employed me, but I also owe it to the area that I am living in.

●●

Wool and wallpaper – ordinary things which you'd think would be easy enough to find – but it's not turning out to be that simple. Thin knitting wool needed to repair a favourite sweater (a dying art as hardly anyone bothers to mend things now – "throw it out and get another" seems to be the common attitude) but where to buy it? Debenham's don't sell wool any longer, Woolworth's might – try there, only a few balls of baby wool – no good. It's Tuesday, there's a stall in the market – this is only half the size it used to be and has much less choice, nothing here that's right. To Winchester Street for the only remaining traditional wool shop in Salisbury – Knit 'n' Needles. At last a decent selection of knitting wool, not quite the right colour but something that will do.

Now for wallpaper – a few weeks ago FADS in Bridge Street might well have had something but they're closing at the end of this month so the selection is limited and nothing is suitable. This is the last city centre decorating shop – a comfortable size, convenient for popping into while in town for other reasons and where, if I did find wallpaper I liked, I could bring it home a small amount at a time on the bus as I made my usual trips home.

Is there anywhere else? Teed DIY in Fisherton Street sells varnishes and stains as does Cross Keys Hardware and Robert Dyas ironmongers and I noticed that Woolworths have paint, brushes, fillers etc – but no wallpaper anywhere. Laura Ashley perhaps – upstairs and no lift – not so convenient for those of us with substandard knees. Quite a good selection of wallpaper but all smooth surfaced, ok for houses with perfect walls but not for those with uneven plaster.

Which only leaves Home Base and B&Q, both out on the Southampton Road, and easy to get to I'm told – yes, if you own a car, but not if you don't. There are buses (X7 to Southampton, 34 & 36 to Alderbury) about once an hour during weekdays, fewer in the evenings and only three on Sundays, but it means crossing a busy road which seems to have little provision for the needs of pedestrians. Buses into Salisbury are easier – B2 from Pauls Dene three times an hour weekdays (none after about 1830 hours or on Sundays). Amesbury buses run, four an hour on weekdays, fewer in the evenings, once an hour on Sundays, fares are 60p into town and 60p again out to the Southampton Road - £2.40 round trip.

But it's not really practical to think of that – carrying home paste and eight rolls of wallpaper single handed isn't possible. Perhaps a taxi would be the thing, how much? About £3.50 each way, home to shops, was the answer, pretty expensive just to buy paper. Choosing wallpaper is always hard, now finding any to choose from has got that way too.

Fenella Kennedy, age 10

Hello, my name is Fenella Kennedy, I am ten years old. Do you want to know about my life in Wiltshire? Here it is.

My usual day is very long and tiring but here it is anyway. I get up at 7.00 a.m. and get breakfast, I also plug my ears to Mum and Dad. This is a good time to fight with my brother, Giles. At 8:25 I go and wait at the bus stop for the school bus. School has a regular timetable to show us what lessons we are coming into, then home again and off to one of various leisure activities.

I like Wiltshire a lot and one of the reasons I like it is because it is a big community. Take Winterslow for example; it has lunch for senior citizens so people can come and have lunch with the pupils and be entertained for a short period afterwards. There is one flaw though: Wiltshire bus company should get the school bus here *on time!* So many times I have been late because of it. Don't laugh: it's not funny. Thankfully we always get home on time, so it is easy to make way for clubs.

There is a lot to do in Wiltshire: including swimming, dancing, riding, sports, and loads more. I wonder if you would be interested in any of these yourself? I take part in dancing and music, which I very much enjoy.

Here comes something particular to one person: friends; my best friends are called: Hannah Clarke, Kate Ryan and Vicky Shepherd. We are always falling out and making up, but sometimes they are too friendly and I can't get away.

Wiltshire is very nice to live in because of the countryside: farms speckle rolling fields and rivers wind their way like long blue snakes; and those areas that are towns and villages, cities, and hamlets, are pretty and spacious. Making my life in Wiltshire a very nice one indeed.

David Kershaw

My name is David Kershaw, the year is 1999AD. I am 13 years-old, and I live in Great Bedwyn, a small village seven miles from Marlborough. I, unlike most of those around me, find the small village boring, as a year ago I was moved from a town. However, I have come to terms with myself and have found the village quite amusing with activities such as tennis and bike-riding.

Tennis is a sport where you have to hit a small ball to an opponent who will then try to hit it back to you, in return you will try to do the same, then him, then you. Until someone does not hit the ball, at which point the other person shall get a point. A bike is an object powered by your feet; you use your feet to turn pedals, the force then travels through a chain to turn a round rubber object known as a wheel.

One thing that particularly interests me is a computer. These are objects full of wires, microchips and resistors, which send information from a mouse (a small scrolling device) or keyboard (a board with buttons) — both controlled by a human user — then this information is processed and you can hear or see the information using a speaker or monitor. Computers can also be linked up to the internet which is a massive collection of millions of computers (give or take) all linked together by the phone system. The phone system has many lines and its primary use is as a communication device for two people.

The other technological machine that I personally love is the T.V. (television); this is a one way communication visual and audio device. That is what it is almost never used for, it is mostly used for the broadcasting of entertainment programmes such as 'Friends', 'Frasier', 'Red Dwarf' and many others. This is also used to tell people the news. The titles of today include the marriage of Prince Edward and Sophie Rhys Jones and the Kosovo Crisis. The T.V. is changing from analogue to digital, this is a secret plan developed by T.V. manufacturers pressuring us into wasting our money and getting a load of rubbish channels. There are even threats that they will turn off the existing T.V. set-up by the year 2010.

I consider my life to be quite good even though there are some troubles in other regions of the world.

Sean Kerwin, age 10

Wiltshire is a south-western point of England. When I moved to Wiltshire from Cornwall I thought it was different. The church is nice because it makes the village a village. Wiltshire is known for its rich farmlands. It has large areas of chalk and uplands separated by the White Horse.

Adam Kington, age 11

The village I live in is called Limpley Stoke. In Lower Stoke the main road is used as a short cut to Bath and Bradford. Our dog Berry has to be taken for walks two times a day. We usually take him down the field by our house, but if we have time to waste we would drive out to a location and walk back home.

The village is mostly for houses but there are some places of work like the hotel, Post Office, pub and down the field is a sewage farm and a small train station. The village is pretty and the children can go pretty much anywhere without having to tell their parents (except private property).

To talk about new developments here would be pretty difficult to me because to my knowledge no major change has accrued save Max a boy next door (and life-long friend) has started secondary school.

In three months I too shall start secondary school. The village is perhaps a bit sleepy but it allows you to muck about which I like to do. School is pretty good but when you are just about to enter secondary school you sometimes think, "Yeah this is nice, but I've done it before; I want something new." Like on Friday we did some algebra and it was really fun.

My family and I like to go to two places for food, clothes etc.

1. Bath because it has lots of shops and it is quite old.

2. Bradford-on-Avon because it has good quality shops (though fewer) and it is quite nice to look at.

In a few weeks my family and I will go to Spain with Max and his family. A week after that I will go to stay with my cousins for two weeks (that's an eight-hour flight by myself!)

Ann Knight

I live and work in Warminster and have done most of my life. I am married and have two children, and am 42 years old. I work as a Library Assistant at Warminster Library and have worked in libraries since I left school at 16. I have seen many changes in that time, mainly going from the old Browne filing system to modern computer capable of holding so much information. I still feel though, that the most important part of my job is human contact, a smile and "Good morning, how are you?" means a lot to our older customers.

Growing up in Warminster in the 1960s I could walk through the Market Place and know most people I met, today with a large Army presence and many new housing estates it's a different story. This is why I feel the town has lost its 'cared for look' – everyone thinks someone else will sort/do that and no-one does. I am proud to live in Warminster and would like to see the small shops and businesses survive against bigger out of town stores.

My children attend Kingdown School, the comprehensive school in Woodcock Road. I was a pupil there from 1969-1973; it must have trebled in size in that time and now has 1,300 pupils on roll. The children are so lucky to have the opportunities and facilities there. A major new block housing music and drama studios and a Sixth Form suite was opened last year. I am secretary to the Kingdown Parent Teacher Association; it is a sign of the times that without raising funds for the school many new computers, books etc., would not be bought. The school financial budget seems to get hit every year. We have raised nearly £4,000 this year for the school.

My husband Paul and son Sam look after sheep as a hobby. We have some land at Crockerton, it is a lovely spot on the edge of the Longleat Estate. They had 24 lambs born in March and have just sold 12 at Frome Market, Standerwick. The field had just been cut for hay and is a lovely place to be. We very often cycle up Bradley Road to Crockerton of an evening and are so lucky with the beautiful countryside. On a Monday evening I play badminton at Warminster School sports hall; I'm not terribly good but I enjoy the social side as we have a lot of laughs.

As I sit in the garden writing this (July 1999 has been very hot) I am listening to Warminster Community Radio, they are on air for a month for which they need a special licence. They do a grand job promoting the town and spreading the community spirit.

Everyone is excited about the Eclipse that is taking place on August 11th, Warminster should have about 98% coverage. There are various commercial purchases you buy – special glasses, T-shirts, that's another sign of the commercial 90s; any event could be a marketing chance!

I look forward to the new millennium, wishing everyone happiness and a wish for peace throughout the world.

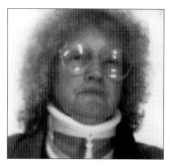

Life, in 1999, is getting easier for people who have disabilities. The Equal Opportunities Policies and the Disability Discrimination Act have begun to ease the problems experienced by people who have all kinds of disability.

Living in a rural area, at Amesbury, on the borders of Salisbury Plain, means having the best of everything. The countryside all around, with the coast only one to one and a half hours away, and quite close to several large towns and cities.

There are many leisure, social and activity groups available to suit all interests and tastes, whether to increase your educational knowledge or learn another language. Everyone has the choice to lead the kind of life they would like. There are many varied opportunities to learn new skills and progress further. Education is available to everyone; it can be a part-time college course, an open learning course, distance learning or an Open University Degree. Numerous social groups cater for every possible interest, culture, belief and ability. The young and not so young can find a club or group to meet their needs.

People who have disabilities are able to go to special groups that cater for their particular disability or to clubs, groups and centres that are provided for all people with any type of disability. The only one of its kind in Wiltshire, Amesbury Activity Centre provides structured groups for people with all types of disabilities. A happy, cheerful and industrious establishment where clients participate in crafts, gardening, swimming, art or the other activities offered. It has been a lifeline for me, and has given me confidence and a positive attitude towards my disability. This increased confidence enabled me to undertake a distance learning course with the University of Wales and train as a volunteer Arthritis Care home visitor.

Facilities are available for people who have disabilities including specially adapted toilets and drop-down kerbs at strategic points on pavements. The local bus company is gradually introducing low-level buses that make wheelchair access possible and these are also useful to people with mobility difficulties and mothers with pushchairs. Many shops now have electronically opening doors, which is another great help and most have ramps or level access. In the home, there are many gadgets available to make life easier for people with disabilities. These go a long way to help people keep their independence for as long as possible. You have the freedom to live your life as you wish.

A great asset to Salisbury is the Shop Mobility Scheme, where electric scooters, electric-wheelchairs and manual chairs can be hired. Another bonus helping towards independence.

Life in 1999 has many opportunities for people who have disabilities, especially if they have a positive attitude and will-power. Things will get even easier for these people in the twenty-first century as more technology is introduced. This will give them more freedom and choice in their lives.

Cathy Lazarus

I like to rise early about 6.30am. I do the washing (take it out of the machine and put it into the tumble dryer). I then make up my two boys' packed lunches. They do not like school dinners. Some things never change!

My Oliver is 10 and goes to the village primary school, St. Mary's, at which there are 49 children. Anton is 11 and goes to John of Gaunt school in Trowbridge.

I ride my bike to work at the village pre-school. The pre-school is adjacent to St. Mary's. This is really good because we have a good working and social relationship with the school. The Head, Mr Kirk, lets me use his photocopy machine and now they have a laminator which I use to preserve the children's work and pictures I wish to keep for the walls.

Gill and I are joint supervisors and we have twelve children on register. The children are from Steeple Ashton, Keevil, Trowbridge and one from Melksham. They are aged from three to four. I finish work around 2pm. There is a lot of paper work as well as cleaning up to do after the children have gone. I cycle home. Past the pub, which is now a Post Office, and carrying on past the lock-up on the green and past the closed down shop. Losing the shop was very sad. It was a focal point for the village. A place to chat, a lifeline for the old and of course ideal for the things you always run out of (bread, milk, sugar, soap).

Back at my house for late lunch. If the weather is cold I have soup, other times a sandwich. I live in a 300 year-old listed cottage. It's beautiful, with natural beams and wonky walls. We have bottled gas for the cooking and heating and a real coal fire in the living room.

I now have about an hour before my Oliver comes home from school. I quickly run round with the Hoover and then if the weather is nice do some gardening.

Oliver arrives home with friends from school. I make them drinks and snacks. The local bus brings Anton home for 4.25, which is 90% reliable for being on time. I prepare tea. If their dad is working at home we eat around 5.30-6pm. This gives us the chance to talk about the day's events.

Tonight I have a meeting at the village school to discuss fund-raising and the teachers give their report as to how things are going in the school and what the school needs, i.e. playground equipment, money towards coach trips or redecorating the class room. The meeting started at 7.30pm and finished at 9pm so a few of us went to the pub after. After a few rounds of drinks and some chips I arrived home before 11pm. Did the usual in the bathroom and went to bed.

My name is Chloe Lee and I live in a small village called All Cannings. The cul de sac that I live in consists of houses and a pig farm. Along the road there is a small shop, a village hall, a pub and a public telephone. The village once had its own bakery but this closed down. It has now been restored and has been turned into a photographic studio called The Bakehouse.

The village has a cricket and a football team which are currently doing very well. The football team had their 1999 end-of-season tour to Holland and won all their matches. The cricket team have a full season of fixtures arranged and hope to win as many of them as possible. All our neighbours keep themselves to themselves and are very pleasant to live around.

During a school week I have to get up at six-thirty in the morning and I catch the bus at seven-thirty. I then spend a day at school, which is called Dauntsey's. We do many activities and sport, I am in the hockey and netball team and I really enjoy both. After all this I catch the bus and I return home at six in the evening.

My hobby is horse riding and I spend quite a lot of my time doing this. I think it is important to have a hobby in the country because it keeps me occupied. I have one older brother and one younger sister. I am glad I have them because when I was very young they were nice to play games with. I also have a dog called Millie and a horse called Boe.

My best friends are Julia Hale and Lucie McNichol. We all have a lot of things in common and I enjoy being with them.

I think that gradually our village will become more built-up because even now there are new houses being built on what used to be a field and we have a new school which replaces the Victorian one. The town nearest to us, Devizes, has become more industrialised and will definitely get bigger as people want more shops and facilities.

When I leave school I plan to be a vet because I love animals. I am optimistic about the future and I hope I am successful in my ambitions and that the next few years are good ones.

Industry, towns and jobs are becoming more developed every day. People are asking for more facilities in the towns, especially the younger generation. Because peoples' jobs are paying well, some people are able to afford a house in the country as well as the town, therefore villages are getting bigger. For example, take the village of All Cannings. Lots of new houses are being built over a field and a new school has been constructed, the bakery has been converted into a photographic studio.

I disagree with the building of houses in our village because it is a really good size at the moment. If we carry on building houses and filling up all the gaps then in a hundred years time we are not going to have much countryside left but in a way more houses are good because it means less people will be homeless.

Most families have a car and some have more than one. When the village was sited nobody had cars. There is evidence that over the past few decades the amount of traffic has increased. Now houses are of a better size and people's living conditions are better. I expect All Cannings and all the other towns and villages to grow during the next century and I think a lot of countryside will be destroyed because of it.

Because there is a growth in industry, businesses and large towns, villages are turning into dormitories where people live and then commute to work. The old village style of life is disappearing because it was based on rural activities. Village houses are in demand, they are expensive and local people are being forced out because rural wages are lower than wages from the town. For this to be reversed the council needs to provide more rural low-cost homes and this puts pressure on rural community and housing expansion continues. There are some benefits in this growth in that the extra people in the villages help to maintain local facilities such as local schools, playgroups, shops, post offices and pubs. In order for the village community to survive they need this population growth.

Mrs Betty Lewis

My life in Wiltshire approaches the idyllic. Though not a native the association goes back to childhood. My parents brought me down from Yorkshire to spend long summers on the farms of three uncles, all in different areas of the country, all beautiful.

The summer was crooning wood pigeons, grasshoppers, the scent of hot sun on bleached grass, apples from old trees. Little did I know that life's roulette wheel would spin and I would slot into one of the areas I loved as a child.

I live in Sherrington in the Wylye Valley. On one side rises the Cleeve, slopes decked with orchids in early summer, later carpeted with downland flowers and at magic moments starred with glow-worms. On the other side the village is bounded by the river Wylye, slipping beneath its footbridge and with willows trailing green fingers.

There is no pub, no shop and the beautiful medieval church is no longer the hub of the community, though still used – and we attend, at Christmas we sing carols round the village. The village numbers about fifty-five souls, employments are diverse and so very different from earlier years. There are employees of the landowner and farmer (resident in another village), two people own farms in other areas. The car enables people to work further afield.

There are three weekend families and a number of the retired. Only two villagers were born in the area. I too am now retired but prior to that worked for the MOD in Warminster – a big source of employment in the area. This necessitated a drive of fifteen minutes. I accompanied my husband – ex-Army employed as a Retired Officer and our two dogs – the Army loves its dogs! At lunch time we could change and walk the dogs on surrounding farm land. Sometimes in summer I would cycle in along the minor road (40 minutes). Delightful ride back at the end of the day, scents of field and garden, perhaps taking an apple from a roadside box.

Some of my leisure activities involve my husband. He is an ornithologist, I sometimes accompany him on field work. I love to walk, mostly alone with the dogs, sometimes with friends. In May I walk the Sarsen Trail Marathon Avebury to Stonehenge, but an average daily walk is one and a half to two hours either in the Great Ridge (wonderful mixed woodland with endless tracks that invite) or on the Plain itself. Here the winter wind has teeth and the rain whips but in summer cloud shadows chase over glossy grass and the sky larks bubble overhead.

I sing in a choir – two concerts a year. I attend concerts in Salisbury Cathedral. We go to theatres in Salisbury, Bath or Bristol, cinema in Salisbury. I love to read. I enjoy cooking for friends and eating out. We have four children, six grandchildren who visit and sometimes stay.

We both garden – a delight, swans fly over, buzzards wheel, small birds throng. But the world intrudes – traffic thunders, jets roar, and strimmers whine. Nonetheless great beauty, a charmed life.

Cilla Liddington

I was born in Back Street, Sherston in 1953. My father's family have lived in this same street for over 400 years.

I met my husband Alan soon after I left school and we married in 1971 when I was just 18. Our first child Max was born two years later followed by Gary and then our daughter Tamara.

In 1996 I achieved my dream of writing and publishing a book about Sherston and am currently working on a second. I have many interests, mainly family and local history. I also update the Internet Web page for the Wiltshire Family History Society of which I am a member.

On the subject of local history I often think things really don't change much in this village. Last week was a good example... Saturday: I was awake at 5.30am ready to go to work at the local factory that produces narrow fabrics for the lingerie trade. This factory is now owned by the Tubbs group and employs many people from the village, as did its predecessor Joseph Davenport in the 1880's.

That same Saturday the village was holding its annual Boules Tournament helping to raise money for the Church, Village Hall and local community. The Church Ale Feast held centuries ago had the same idea. That night we danced to music in the school field, not in the High Street as in the 1930's when the Penny Hop dances where held.

Sunday was a lovely hot and sunny day. After lunch with my family we took our two dogs for a walk along the River Avon. In the evening the Salvation Army band held an open-air service of Thanksgiving in the

High Street on the same site that Samuel Stubbings, a travelling Baptist minister, held his open-air prayer meetings in 1840.

Monday: Parish Council meeting. Decisions were made on whether to preserve an ancient right of way and to discuss planning applications. Did the Lord of the Manor have to make such decisions at his Court Leet in the village in the 1700s?

Tuesday: Catching up with correspondence, not by penny post but by the marvels of the Internet. Within minutes my letters and photographs of the Boules day are whizzing around the world to family and friends.

Wednesday: The afternoon is spent on my favourite hobby, genealogy. With all the modern technology on offer I can use my computer to chart and print out my family history.

Thursday: Into Malmesbury today to buy groceries from the supermarket. I have them delivered to my door, but then again Billy Camm made home deliveries on his horse and trap to my great grandmother's house years ago.

Friday: The vacuum cleaner comes out. With two dogs, two cats and three children, I think the old-fashioned carpet sweeper of my mother's would make little impression! In the evening I settle down with a glass of wine to reflect on a busy week in Sherston.

Danny Lucas, age 10

I have lived in Wiltshire all my life and I love the green and countryside and the rich farmers' land and birds of prey flying near our school, farmers ploughing their ground and I would not like to move because I have plenty of friends. My favourite sports are tennis and a bit of football. My hobbies are farming. My places of interest are Stonehenge and West Kennet Long Barrow.

Eight-thirty. The post office is ready for business but there's no one about. It's very quiet! I am already thinking that after closing at 4.30 tonight, the account for the past week has to be prepared, so, during today I must check my paperwork and assemble the many different forms. It is not such an onerous task as it might appear – business in a village of just 180 households is not great and, sad to say, it is diminishing – it has been for the past decade. The core of Post Office business has always been handling pensions and child benefits – cash over the counter – but the numbers of pensioners and new mums opting for this method of payment falls each year, they are of the new age, 'hole in the wall', telephone banking, direct debits and standing orders. Hard cash does not figure highly in their financial thoughts. Still, some, who value the presence of the Post Office for the other things it offers, do draw cash, even one lady who could probably buy the whole village if she wanted to – she recognizes the wider social value of my 12ft by 9ft office.

Fifteen minutes after opening. Signs of life. Mums and children walking to the village school, if the children spot me standing at the door they wave – they call me by my first name, even the toddlers – it's nice. One or two of the mums will call in on the way back from school, I shall sell a few stamps, a greetings card perhaps or probably it will be a discussion on some aspect of the village – the fête, the hall, the parish council - I get involved in all of these.

Our postlady, having finished her deliveries, drops in a yellow pouch with items to go back to the main delivery office in Salisbury. It will be picked up by the Royal Mail van driver as he empties the letter boxes through the valley. He should empty the letter box at my office at 9.15 but we all know that it will be well past ten before he appears. It's sunny today so he'll definitely be in shorts.

Eleven o'clock and the office is full – that's not difficult – four customers constitutes a crowd in my small office. In between the conversations I manage to squeeze in one or two transactions! Not many more come in before I close for lunch. Back to work, the lady I've just served was born and raised in the village, I remember her as a happy schoolgirl buying penny sweets. Now she is a happy and capable mum with a girl and twin boys.

There is a routine in village life, different people come in at different times on different days, if they don't, and they are elderly or live alone, a discreet enquiry will determine if all is well with them. Today I am about to check on one lady but it's all right, I remember she told me she is going on holiday with her daughter. I close on the dot and get down to the accounts. They balance, well nearly! In the early part of the year 2000 my office is to be equipped with a computer system, they say it will open up new avenues of business – I hope it does.

Rebecca McKee, age 10

I first moved to Wiltshire at the age of six. I had moved from a town so life in a village was different. There were lots of fields that Dad liked to walk through. There were lots more houses in the town, but the houses in the town were smaller and the gardens were smaller.

I made one or two friends with people who live down my road. I've lived in Dilton Marsh (a small Wiltshire village), for a few years and in that time I've made friends with lots of people, and I've argued with friends and friends have moved house.

Whenever visitors visit us, we take them up to see the White Horse. I like Avebury because there are lots of stones to climb up and shops to buy things from. There are lots of beautiful scenery. There are lots of historical houses with beams that are about 200 years-old. I'll never forget my life in Dilton ... even if something will change after the millennium.

Deepantar Majumdar, age 13

My name is Deepankar Majumdar and I am an average thirteen-year-old boy. I have an average family, in an average home, with an average routine. I live in Swindon, Wiltshire. Swindon's founder was Isambard Kingdom Brunel, who was a famous railway engineer. He built Swindon as a railway town. It quickly became the fastest growing town in the country.

Those were the days when you could enjoy a relaxing day watching the trains go by. But that was years and years ago. Now, the trains are unreliable and instead of railways there are office blocks and factories on the skyline. But I never stated that that was all bad.

Swindon is now the centre of business for Wiltshire. It has huge factories of the Japanese and French car manufacturers, Honda and Renault. It is also home to EMI records and Nationwide Building Society, both are the two most stunning modern buildings in Wiltshire.

There is also much more to do if you are young, like me. There are three swimming pools, an ice rink, about eight leisure centres, a 16,000 seater football stadium, a bowling alley, two modern cinemas, four large shopping centres, three McDonalds and a Pizza hut, which are two of the best loved fast food restaurants in the world.

The community is nice, too. Swindon is a place full of many races, cultures and religions. My parents, who are both Asian, therefore found it easy to settle in. People respect each other here, and that is good. For those people who don't like living life on the fast highway of the city, the surrounding area may whet your appetite. Wiltshire is full of good, fresh, country air, there are flowers, and a few weeds (unlike at home — my mother takes great pride in her garden). There is wildlife, and all other aspects of nature. The people that live around here are mostly farmers, they grow crops or farm animals to use as food or to sell off for income.

Wiltshire is a county of many landmarks. The white chalk horse stands proudly on the hill, the ancient stones at Avebury attract public from all over the world, and Silbury Hill has puzzled archaeologists.

For the millennium, Swindon might achieve city status. That would be brilliant. Swindon may be large and noisy, but the countryside makes it better.

There is a church-based village magazine which incorporates many aspects of village life, this is delivered voluntarily to every home in the village itself and surrounding smaller villages (3,000 copies). There is one main village noticeboard owned and managed by the Parish Council which advertises local events as they occur. Noticeboards are also *in situ* outside the local churches, Scout Hall and in the village hall.

The village hall (Bouverie Hall) is exceptionally well used by the local community for WI Market, Day Care, Dance Club, WI meetings, the extremely popular Gardening Club which has speakers every month in winter and outings every month in summer, public meetings, social events, pantomime, amateur dramatic productions, private functions, church functions, choral productions.

Pewsey becomes a focal point for two weeks in September with differing events taking place each evening e.g. dramatic productions, skittles, water events, Beer race, Pub Games, Shop Window competition, sport orientated events, quizzes, dances, choirs, outdoor church services, discos, fair etc. culminating in illuminated evening procession on the third Saturday in September.

The Scotchel Nature Reserve belongs to and is managed by the Parish Council, the local Primary School is involved in an ongoing River Watch monitoring river levels, water colour, plant, animal and bird life, etc. The Rectory Grove is a conservation area near the village centre owned and managed by the Parish Council. There is a large wetland area near the canal owned and managed by the Wiltshire Wildlife Trust. Footpaths and bridleways are kept clear in most cases by the Parish Council, and using volunteer parishioners, but also on a few footpaths the Probationary Service carries out community service work.

Since the opening of the new CRS Pioneer supermarket in May 1997, local retail businesses have had to think on their feet and diversify in order to keep going, this has meant a wider variety of items available and as a spin off services available to the general public. Most local businesses support the community totally, especially at Carnival time in September when many events are staged incorporating businesses. Many people are employed locally in a wide variety of business enterprises. The Community Craft & Tea Room is an excellent example of local people working specifically for the community at no personal gain, as is staffing the tea shop at Pewsey Wharf.

There are various pre-school playgroups in the village including Little Fishes run by the local Anglican church and Puddleducks playgroup and creche available at Pewsey Sports Centre, for parents using the sports facilities as well as an open playgroup. A youth group meets at The Shak within the Sports Centre and Crusaders in the Anglican Church Room within the actual church building. Uniformed youth organisations are also active within the village e.g. Brownies, Guides, Beavers, Cub Scouts, Scouts, Venture Scouts, Red Cross. Youth Sports have a high profile, e.g. football, including eight successful Youth Football Teams, Tennis, with over a hundred keen youngsters involved, Running Club, whose younger members compete on a wide scale nationally and in some cases internationally, Swimming Club, with a large membership.

Pewsey Link, a volunteer group, has been running for several years and is in the main used by older people to transport them to hospital, appointments, shopping etc. Home helps are organised by social services. A volunteer Day Care Centre operates weekly and regular trips are arranged through the locally run Evergreen Club. Sports for older people are actively encouraged at the Sports Centre specifically with Over 50 sessions. The Bowls Club has a large number of older members. Pewsey Older People group meets regularly and local issues are addressed through speakers and discussion. Many senior citizens are involved in the various village activities which take place e.g. local clubs and societies.

My name is Catherine Meeke and I am 13 years-old. My birthday is on 7th June and I was born in York.

I live in Tidworth. Tidworth is a garrison town and we live here because my father is in the Army. My mother writes a newsletter called Drumbeat which is delivered to people in Tidworth, Bulford and Netheravon.

The emblem of Tidworth is a drummer, the 'Tedworth Drummer'. A couple of centuries ago a man called William Drury travelled around, beating his drum and collecting money. One day when he was in Ludgershall he was arrested for not having a licence for his drum and it was therefore confiscated by the Magistrate. Drury was tried, found guilty and put in jail where he later died. After his death the drum started beating by itself at night, causing great consternation to the Magistrate and his family. The emblem of Tidworth has been a drummer ever since.

There are lots of good things to do in Tidworth. There is a brand new Astroturf, used for playing hockey and the Oval for Athletics. There is a library, a swimming pool, and next summer we will have a new Leisure Centre too. There is also the Garrison itself - which is not always a good thing because of the tanks which rumble past your window at 5 o'clock in the morning!

Tidworth's population is made up of Army and civilian people who live side by side in the town. The Army is the largest part of the population but it is transitory, which means that the number remains the same but the people come and go. Most of the civilian population have been in the Army in the past and liked Tidworth so much that they stayed.

According to statistics, Wiltshire is the safest county in England. It is split into three areas and Tidworth is in the Salisbury area which is the safest of all of them. Crime is very low in Tidworth because we have three police forces here: Wiltshire Constabulary, the Ministry of Defence Police and the Royal Military Police. They all work together very well to stop crime. I live in the safest place in England !

I hope you liked hearing about Tidworth. I enjoy living there because it is an exciting place to live because things are always happening.

Life at the turn of the Century

I am sitting here, in the third row from the back, chewing my pen lid. My teacher is sitting talking to a pupil behind me. Our class is small with only 19 pupils. I don't know quite what I'm going to write for this book for the end of the millennium but I'll give it my best shot.

My name is Georgina Aline Miller and I'm twelve years old. I live in a tiny out-in-the-sticks place called Bratton. The best things about Bratton are that it's pretty, clean and in the middle of the countryside. There isn't much litter and there are two recreational areas. I live in a brick and stone, detached house right at the end of my village, so from my bedroom I can see fields surrounded by hedges with cows grazing. It's changed so much over the years that when I look at photos I hardly recognize it. Half of my street was fields and most of the estates were not there.

The school only had three classrooms. There was a staff room which doubled as an office. Two of the classes had a folding wall which was opened to allow a stage entrance for any plays or just to have a bigger classroom. The school dinners were delivered and all sports were played outside. The school will continue to change with the introduction of a mobile classroom at the end of the millennium. I'd like my village to stay the same size but to have more sophisticated transport links and more things for children to do. I used to walk to my primary school. Pupils have to catch a coach to any local secondary school in the district including me.

I regard myself as lucky. When I think about people living on the streets nowadays this makes me appreciate what I've got. I have great opportunities and some people will never have the chance to do half the things I've done in the past. My secondary school is a public school called Dauntsey's in West Lavington. Public schools are often regarded as having a better standard of education than state schools. I think this is unfair. Everyone should have the chance to have an excellent education regardless of wealth. The Labour government abolished the Assisted Places Scheme toward the end of the millennium and this widens the gap between state and private schools even more.

I have lived in Trowbridge all my life, I have lived in Melksham all my life as well. I think that it is the scumyest town in Wiltshire but I don't want to move because of all my friends, they just live over the road.

My favourite sports are football and BMXing (British motor cross) me and my friends make jumps anywhere we can. I play for my school team as a goalkeeper.

Wiltshire has some of the best sites for visiting in Great Britain. It has the most heritage sites, e.g. Stonehenge, Avebury, but I do wish the Council would put in some more BMX tracks and jumps because I am bored of making jumps that get ruined by other people.

There are lots of places to go, e.g. cinemas, bowling alleys etc.

Gillian Minter

From my top-floor eighteenth-century home I share with swooping house martins an aerial view of twentieth-century Chippenham at play. On the Avon below, canoeists in yellow life-jackets practise capsize drill. The new sky-blue bridge, a link in the developing national cycleway, attracts children to paddle and walkers to contemplate waterfowl and fishermen.

Around the house lies a public golf-course where would-be Tiger Woods in baseball caps and trainers belt orange balls into our purple lavender, startling squirrels. Towards the station, through which since privatisation pass a plethora of trains of varying promptness, and before the Leisure Centre offering everything from judo to aerobics, is Monkton

Park, our house's former estate and now home to junior football, funfairs, shows, Folk Festival, Guy Fawkes bonfire, Carnival fireworks, campers. Adults walk dogs and the young embrace on the grassy slopes.

We have another estate now – of red and pink housing which doesn't fit with local stone and blocks our view of dinghy sails in the meadow. This reflects government policy to Build More Houses. A new school is planned on the field beyond, where World War II bombs were recently detonated. Monkton House, which once had formal gardens and a wharf to cross by boat to church, will see more changes in the coming century.

Meanwhile, I enjoy retirement. Tennis, rambling and swimming (for the over-50s) theoretically benefit my ageing physique. My mind is stimulated by language groups of the local U3A [University of the Third Age] and Twinning Association; and by travel to our twin towns or more exotic destinations inaccessible within a working leave allowance. I take daytrips; my ration of Senior Citizen travel tokens from the District Council comes in handy. I sing, somewhat flat, in a Ladies' Choir, and practise painting at Chippenham College.

To our Community I give a little back as Governor of a primary school grappling with initiatives on literacy, numeracy and information technology. Producing the Talking Newspaper for the Blind occupies occasional mornings: local news is much as in my youth, though with more violence. I give talks at Day Centres where elderly ladies doze. I serve on committees of groups sharing an increasing problem in attracting young members.

There's plenty to do. I'm thankful to be in the pre-war age group of women with a State Pension entitlement at 60; born later, I'd have to wait till 65. TV is seductive, though I eschew satellite TV, email and the Internet.

On summer evenings, I open my sash windows and absorb the peace of the shadowy park. Owls hoot; teenagers giggle. The sounds of traffic, readmitted at 7.30 to the pedestrianised High Street, are muffled by old buildings and the parish church whose illuminated spire glows against the night sky. Bats flit past. Life in Chippenham is good in 1999.

I live in the north-west part of Wiltshire in a small village called Brinkworth. It was once (or still is) one of the longest villages in England. I'm 11 years old and my birthday is on 20th March. I was born in 1988 at Princess Margaret Hospital in Swindon. I go to Brinkworth Earl Danby's Primary School which is in our village, my best friend is Felicity Hill. My school starts at 8.45 a.m. and ends at 3.15 p.m. In the morning we have quick number, spellings and sometimes assembly. At 10.30 am we have a playtime and lunch at 12.00. My teacher is Mrs. Scanlon. Our last topic was Britain in the 1930s. I belong to a gang called the Fred on Toast Gang. I sit on Table 3 who are made up of Ben who lives for Star Wars and Warhammer, Felicity who loves cats, James who supports Arsenal, Mark who likes reading, Sarah who likes playing with her friends, Zara who likes playing netball and Jonathan who doesn't really like working. My family are my dad Rob, my mum Kate and my sister Hannah. My pets are my two cats called Jess and Boots, my two rats called Sally and Kelly and about twenty stick insects.

We shop in Chippenham in Safeway. Every Saturday I get £2 pocket money. In September 1999 I'll go to Filands which is the secondary school for this area. The good entertainment around here is: Cotswold Wildlife Park and Water Park, Longleat which is another wildlife park and our Virgin and Cineworld cinemas. Oh, and I musn't forget the swimming pools – Wootton Bassett, Swindon, Chippenham and Malmesbury. Malmesbury is an outdoor pool. While on the subject of swimming I'll tell you about one of my hobbies. I love swimming! I'm a Wootton Bassett Otter which is one of the teams for this area. I swim every Friday and Sunday and in Galas some Saturdays. I support Southampton FC who just esaped relegation this season. I don't really like Manchester United, Arsenal or Everton but everyone's different! My other hobby is Guides. I go every Tuesday evening. Next week we are going rock climbing, I'm really excited. We call one of our leaders Blossom and the other Thorn! In the summer and half-terms we go to camp at the Lime Kiln Leisure Centre. We go swimming and play lots of different sports.

I have nine cousins and eleven uncles and aunties. Every summer holiday (we get six weeks) we go camping in Wales or Devon and we have lots of fun.

Life at the turn of the Century   99

Julie Mitten, age 15

An average day in the life of a schoolgirl, aged 15 in Wiltshire. I wake up when my mother wakes me around 7.00 a.m. to get ready for school. I go downstairs and have some cornflakes, coffee and then I return back upstairs to wash and brush my teeth. During this my mother has ironed my school uniform. I get dressed and brush my hair. I pack my bag with my school books and lunch. It's now about 8.25 and at 8.30 I find my shoes and leave the house, scurrying to school to arrive around 9.00 am.

I go to registration then off to my lessons, English, French, Science, History and Spanish. This lasts until 3.40 p.m. when I leave school with my friends slowly walking home via their houses. We arrive in town to look at music or whatever we need to look at. Gradually we split up into groups and go home. At home I make myself a cup of coffee and sit down to watch the children's programmes as my brothers run in and out with their friends, Nathan, Ashley and Alan. My father, out of bed, starts to prepare dinner. At around 5.30 dinner is ready and 'Neighbours' begins. At around 6.00 my sister and her family come around. I then make endless cups of coffee and clean up her toddler daughter. At around 8.00 p.m. they leave and we watch television until 9.30 I then go to my bedroom, get changed and do any homework I have or read a book until 10.30-10.45 p.m. I then go to sleep listening to the radio. The next day it starts over again.

Jane Moody

I live in an almshouse built in 1862 on the site of Fisherton tollgate. It overlooks the place where stood both a gaol and a gibbet. Now, when I look across at the same place, I see a constant fume-emitting carousel of trucks, vans and cars: a traffic roundabout. The almshouse was established to accommodate impoverished widows of the clergy. Conditions of occupation have changed, but licensees, (we are not tenants), must have links with a church. The community consists of twelve ladies, mostly old, but at eighty-two I am far from the oldest.

Eighty-two is a funny age to be. It is often assumed to be a time for living in a special old people's home, feeble-minded and helpless, dribbling and incontinent. This is not so.

There are countless opportunities in Salisbury to continue learning. Just now, the computer is exploding into every aspect of our lives. Fortunately the government has sponsored courses where folk of any age can learn about e-mail, World Wide Web, Internet, etc., and go further with studies if they so wish. I find it fascinating and bewildering, but am happy to no longer be a complete computer idiot.

The library provides unending pleasure. One can spend hours there perusing newspapers, magazines and books. There is a ceaseless output of the written word. However, long dead authors are still my favourites – Thomas Hardy, Charles Dickens, George Eliot. The library also runs a monthly book group. A particular book is read during the preceding month, and later discussed by members. Views are varied so make for diverse and stimulating conversation. In addition, the library exhibits paintings, photographs etc., and is the venue for lectures on differing subjects.

I attend a regular church fellowship meeting. Talks given or slides shown are of a general nature – nothing controversial. A cup of tea, a biscuit, and a word here and there, conclude a gentle afternoon. A weekly lunch for old people is held at the United Reformed Church. Members of various churches cook and wait on us with cheerfulness, courtesy and great kindness.

Walking three or four miles most days is a normal pastime. I belong to a walking group, but prefer going alone. I can observe the strange, the quaint, the general oddities of life. I see earth's beauty. As I write, in May, meadows are yellow with shiny buttercups; horse-chestnut 'candles' stand proudly aloft. But there is sadness. The wonder of 'darkness' is being pushed farther and farther away. Towns grow larger, buildings higher, and public lighting more and more garish, effectively blotting out the sky. Stars and magical moonlight fade.

I well remember my grandmother who was born in 1852. As a child, she told me stories of her own childhood. And my mother, born in 1881 into a world where horses were the only transport, lived long enough to witness on television the first moon landings. The pace of change is indeed awesome.

Sophie Moody

● ●

I am a relatively new person to Wiltshire as my family, namely my husband, myself and my son moved to Amesbury in November 1997. We bought one of the brand new houses being built on the old Boscombe Down sports field. It is now May 1999 and in that short time most of the building work has been completed by the builders Persimmons, Bloors and Wilcon: Gleeson, the last remaining builder, still has quite a few properties to build.

We have been made to feel very welcome here despite moving into new properties which are expanding Amesbury rapidly in size.

Now a little about myself. My name is Sophie. I am thirty-three years old, five foot tall, married and a mother of a two year-old boy called Miles.

When we first moved here I was encouraged by my health visitor to join a local group held at the Amesbury Baptist Church, called Mompower. It is a group designed for mothers with a child under one to meet, talk through problems with a health visitor and each other whilst their babies are looked after in a creche run by members of the church. From this group I met several mothers who I now keep in regular contact with, one of whom has now become the postmistress of Shrewton Post

Office, others have husbands in the Army and some like myself have civilian partners. Les works in Andover for a computer firm.

On Wednesday afternoons Miles and I attend the Shrewton toddler group. Miles plays with the toy cars, climbs on the climbing frame, plays with play doh etc.

On Thursdays I become a working adult for a short time. Miles goes to a local childminder whilst I teach the violin at two schools – Bulford C of E and Woodford Valley. Woodford Valley School had its first violin group set up in September 1998 and we hope to expand to two or more groups in 1999.

I have recently had an interview to become a relief library assistant in the Salisbury area but as yet I have not heard whether I have the post or not.

I joined the Amesbury and Boscombe Down link group to help provide transport to those who need it e.g. for hospital appointments. It has been a wider opportunity to visit a greater spectrum of people. We try to attend St. Mary and St. Melor church when we can.

I enjoy being a mother and living here in Amesbury despite having aircraft flying over at very low altitude, air raid sirens going off during the middle of the night and guns firing on Salisbury Plain.

The people here are very friendly.

Alan Morley

In mid-May, 1999, I stood in the Shires Shopping Centre in Trowbridge watching them dismantle the 'Meccano' clock tower. It had been standing as a symbol of the resurgence of Trowbridge since 1989, a few years later than my residency in the town.

I moved from the Cotswolds in 1986 on taking early retirement when I was 55, and it was to a new relationship. I had met my second wife while I was still living in Stroud, and to share one house seemed not only sensible but desirable, so I pulled up twenty year-old roots and moved forty miles down the A46.

I was not impressed by Trowbridge. It seemed a drab town left marooned by the departure of its industrial past which had receded, leaving it high and dry. Amid the flotsom the great white whale of County Hall stood as if stranded betwixt Salisbury or Devizes.

The shopping centre was Fore Street, Silver Street and the Market, and was not inspiring. The Park was pleasingly unauthoritarian. But to someone with a sense of the past there was a bonus. It was the house I moved into. It had a history, albeit a modest one, and of course my future wife lived there.

This was Dursley House, formerly the home of James Bodman, Trowbridge's first, eccentric, historian. Built in the 1790's it had begun life as a weaver's house with the looms on the third floor. Subsequently it became a farmhouse, and was finally bought by a speculative builder to be partitioned into two 'semis', with four modern houses built, courtyard fashion, in what had been the farmyard. A modest enough property, it still retained its Georgian dignity. It is Grade 2 listed.

Not local, not even thinking of myself as part of the town in which I now lived, nevertheless it aroused all my instincts as a local historian which had been active in Stroud.

I began to look around me and to discover that Trowbridge possessed a certain charm. She had never been beautiful, even 'pretty', but was a lady of character and integrity with whom you could form a respectful relationship while never presuming to a love affair. And what I now found intensely interesting was the restoration process as the old lady was propelled into a new lease of life. As I watched she gradually changed.

First came the Shires development, spearheaded by the Gateway (later Asda) Supermarket, and the clock – a defiant, if controversial, gesture. Then followed the shopping centre of which the town can be proud, not least in the imaginative conversion of Home Mills as a quality museum, a vibrant link with the past.

Nor has it been allowed to become a traffic bottleneck, with County Way (with the Tesco Supermarket) and Bythesea Road channelling the through traffic via the multi traffic-lit Longfield Roundabout which, after some initial confusion and driver hostility, copes very well.

There is hope too of a resurgence in the town's social life with the opening of the Arc Theatre, and the promise of a state of the art entertainment centre and five screen cinema in St. Stephen's Place. On the minus side the Town's football team vanished after a proud history and the 1930's swimming pool went in making way for the new Tesco store, but any change inevitably brings its casualties.

There is, above all, a sense of hope and purpose present in the spirit of Trowbridge that was missing when I came thirteen years ago. The year 2000 should be entered with confidence.

Hayley Mountjoy, age 14

Living in Wiltshire at this particular time of the 20th century is absolutely brilliant. Wiltshire is generally thought of as a quiet, tidy county full of farmers but in actual fact it's got much more to offer than fields.

It has great shops selling food, clothes, shoes, toys, music, magazines, sweets and anything you can imagine.

The people are friendly, helpful and altogether nice. Apart from the odd individual but those kind of people are extremely rare.

Schools are a very important part of life for people age 4-18. Education is absolutely crucial if one wants to be successful in life. If a child does not go to a school then the parent could go to prison and the child must be enrolled in a school immediately.

Lessons include maths, English, science, French, German, Spanish, drama, dance, art technology, P.E. and much more. Punishments include detention, exclusion, and even being expelled, school lasts from Monday to Friday.

Out of school, people my age 'hang out' places, go to discos, clubs, watch television, listen to music, and homework (which nobody really likes much!). Some people ice-skate, ride horses, roller skate, collect things, go to the cinema, read, write; every individual has their own passion.

There are youth clubs to join and the one I go to arranges camping trips in the summer, trips to theme parks, swimming and other fun things. Most of the kids get on very well but do tend to argue once in a while. An enormous part of life is fashion and music. There are different styles of clothes and a new style comes out every season! Every week on the radio, it announces the top 40 selling singles of that week. Pop is the most common type of music I think, but dance, rock, soul, rap and hip-hop are very popular too.

Living near Stonehenge is really cool too as it's a famous landmark and people travel from all around the world to see it and I live 10-15 minutes away from it and my friend can see it from her living room window so that's really ace.

If I had a choice I wouldn't live in any other time zone in any other part of Britain because everything I could possibly want is right here with me.

Dominic Mundy, age 13

Wiltshire was a place only ever visited when I went to see my grandparents who lived in Shrewton, a small village near Stonehenge so it seemed really strange, particularly for Dad when his job moved to Swindon and we all moved to Enford, a tiny hamlet just a few miles from the village in which Dad had been brought up.

For me, since I was 11, it was just the right time to move to secondary school anyway. Stonehenge soon became a familiar sight as we travelled down regularly from Kent to look for houses and visit schools. School was the priority yet I knew as soon as we approached the front entrance to Dauntsey's that the vast playing fields, the astro, the numerous tennis courts and the swimming pool were too inviting and so my choice was easy. I just needed to pass the entrance exam which fortunately I subsequently did.

For my parents finding a suitable house was to prove more of a problem and we initially had to settle for a rented house in Steeple Ashton. Luckily the neighbours welcomed us and we made some really good friends so we were sad to leave this part of Wiltshire when the new house we had decided to buy was finally complete.

I love our new house. The journey to and from school is always interesting seeing so much wildlife as we drive along - foxes, badgers and rabbits are often part of the scenery as well as army tanks and parachutists. A vast difference from the built-up area in which we used to live. Past our local pub, which incidently the villagers own, we reach our brand new house down a narrow country lane. Everyone has made us welcome and tell us what an improvement the house has made to the area since it had been built on a dilapidated old farm site. We have increased the local population to 76.

Mum and Dad are gradually getting the house and the garden just as they want it and I know it will take time but even after just one year, it is very much our Wiltshire home.

Jack Nichols, age 13

I live in Devizes which is a small market town in Wiltshire. There are many sporting activities to do for the young athletes and sports fans. Devizes offers many sporting activities from the basic open space to play in and do your own thing. There is also the Devizes Leisure Centre which has many facilities which include a swimming pool, a sports hall, a gym, outside tennis courts (and if the weather's bad you can play tennis indoors) and playing fields. Along with the leisure centre is Devizes Tennis Club which I am a regular member of, events there are on newly re-done courts.

The Leisure centre offers a variety of clubs including the "Basic" club which is on every Friday evening. For £1 you get the use of the swimming pool and either the sports hall in the winter and the tennis courts in the summer. There are also a few youth clubs like the Bishops Cannings youth club (BACE) (which is on most Sundays, except for holidays, for 50p admission).

I participate in the BACE youth club, Devizes tennis club who I play for regularly when they organise matches with other clubs and Basic if I have hardly any homework. For those who think that shopping is the most exciting thing to do on this planet Devizes won't offer too much in the way of fashion shops and big name brands except for Boots, Woolworths and W.H. Smith which are probably the biggest names there. Staying in the centre of the town and the market place there is a cinema with one screen compared to the other cinemas around it has nothing. There are also many pubs, most of which sell Wadworth brands as Devizes is the home of the Wadworth brewery.

The beer is transported around to the pubs by shire horses as part of tradition. Wiltshire is about the only real Wadworth territory as the brewery is so small.

I think that Devizes is a very nice place to live as it has most of the facilities that you want and has pretty little traffic and it is metres away from peaceful countryside.

Rebecca Oliver, age 11

My name is Rebecca, I am 11 years and 4 months old. I live in north-west Wiltshire. I used to live in Essex but we had to move here. I have a cat, dog, guinea pig, fish and stick insects. My friends at school are Lauren, Sarah, Zara, Emma, Katherine, out of school I have lots more. I haven't got a best friend but some of my friends have. Where I live we have two main towns to get shopping, one is Swindon the other is Wootton Bassett, we normally get our shopping there. My Dad works in Swindon and my Mum works in Princess Margaret's hospital. She is a midwife and a nurse. My sister's in the same class as me, that's very annoying. Going back to my friends, I play skipping with them at play times. Lauren is chubby but very quiet in class but outside she is really loud and Sarah is very noisy but can get a bit mad, Zara is really loud outside but inside she is like Lauren but a bit louder, Zara is the tallest out of us all! Emma and Katherine are best friends, Katherine makes me laugh the most. Emma loves horses and I think she has three. Her mum likes horses too. I like all of my friends the same. Sarah and Zara's parents have both split up. Sometimes Sarah gets really upset about it. Zara lives the closest to me out of all my friends, in fact she only lives down the road. In the mornings and afternoons I catch the bus when I go to Malmesbury School, that's my secondary school. Dizzy is my dog – brother, she is hard to look after! She is a black lab and I love her.

● ●

"I'm growing old," the Walrus said, but although aged 77 I shed no tears, just happy to be in Nettleton after an interesting life. Our village is part of a honeycomb, the apt name of the parish magazine covering Biddestone, Burton, Castle Combe, Grittleton, Leigh Delamere, Slaughterford, West Kington, Littleton Drew and Yatton Keynell. The parish priest, Rachel Lewis, recently invited to preach the sermon in Westminster Abbey, recited all the names for which she and her team are responsible.

Netttleton is not as picturesque as some Wiltshire villages but has a great heart in the shape of a shop and Post Office run with great expertise and charm by Mrs Frank Bell. Our 14th century church has two services a month but our Church of England school has, this very year 1999, joined an amalgamation of several village schools in a lovely new building at Yatton Keynell.

My working day consists of hoping for the excuse of fine weather and gardening with a promise to catch up on housework later. Rain or shine I walk our Staffordshire Bull Terrier morning and evening; collect the milk delivered daily and placed in a tin marked "Bread". Our postman, Alan, is a another vital caller, but it is frequently only advertising material. Friday is a day which has to be remembered as dustbin day, except on Bank Holiday.

We both have bikes, especially useful for trips to the Post Office or to deliver the *Honeycomb* as my husband does. He is also a pigeon fancier and belongs to a club in Chippenham which organises races from as far afield as France. He was a fighter pilot in the Battle of Britain and the Middle East so flight has real meaning for him.

No one driving through Nettleton could know of its hidden talents except for the evidence of two farms with Friesain milk herds. You need to be a resident to know of the guitar maker, the TV criminal court artist, the race horse owner, the furniture maker, the chandelier expert, tennis coach and so on. The prevailing west wind frequently brings balloons overhead in all shapes and sizes and, under their own steam, the enduring Hercules from RAF Lyneham.

Having lived in Africa many miles from anywhere we really appreciate having neighbours and especially their helpfulness – a flat car battery, a hospital appointment and three willing pushers appeared from nowhere

– again a young neighbour rushed to our front door thinking we might have been attacked when he saw a car making a fast getaway down our drive – it was a legitimate 'draught excluder' workman – and again an ex-nursing neighbour knew all that was necessary when my husband became semi-conscious from stings after disturbing a wasps' nest; and he received very prompt and first class medical care from the Chippenham Ambulance Service and the old hospital.

There are small sadnesses like the dying elms after 30 years growth or world-wide horrors daily on our TV so our consolidation and thankfulness is for our four sons and their families even if our grandchildren despair at our lack of computer and fax machine.

Emilia Page, age 11

My name is Emilia and I love living in Wiltshire. I am 11 years old and I moved to Wiltshire from London when I was almost three. Life in Wiltshire is very different from London life. In Wiltshire we can have a big garden and lots of countryside. I love having these because we can play football, take our dog for walks and generally have fun. There are also lots of tracks, woods and paths that I can ride my bike in.

I would like to be a young children's author when I grow up. My favourite author at the moment is Jackie Wilson. On Friday the 4th of June I went to hear her talk as part of the Salisbury Festival and I got her to sign my book. I was inspired by her. Jacqueline Wilson said that she came to Wiltshire because she liked it here. She lives in Somerset, I wonder, what it is like there? I think there must be a lot of bookshops there, she has over 10,000 books. I like reading books as well as writing them, which is good because there are brilliant bookshops in Salisbury, like Waterstones and Ottakars.

I don't do many activities in Winterslow or Salisbury because there are not very many. I like swimming which is lucky because there is a swimming pool in Salisbury. Sometimes I go rollerblading with my family and friends in a park or down our roads or lanes.

I think the community in the village I live in is brilliant. At Winterslow Guides (an outside of school club for girls), if we were going on an outing anywhere and our leader couldn't provide the transport the people would ring each other up and ask if they could share lifts. The people nearly always say yes. I wonder why?

If you live in Wiltshire already and are planning to move don't move to another county stay in Wiltshire!

Matthew Parry, age 12

The small village that I live in, Worton, is a linear village with a river running parallel to the main road like train tracks. The houses and the river, The Millrace, are separated by a spread of fields. The lane leading down to the river is banked by a copse of trees. Standing on the bridge spanning the banks of the Millrace, I look down the lengths and I see trees dipping their branches towards the river as if they were trying to reach the water. Further on is a waterfall leading off into a pool of crystal clear water, the waterfall pounds against the concrete ledges and makes an unearthly din. The river water is glassy clear and I can see fish swimming around on the bottom. Leading off the waterfall is a stream, which is fun to bridge over with dead branches. There is a natural bridge made from an old gnarled oak, which has uprooted itself over the stream thus giving a perfectly useable bridge although the other bank is covered in nettles.

The village has a public house called The Rose and Crown and a primary school which hosts unlimited amounts of fêtes and football contests. The best fête event is the skittles in which you have to propel a hard round ball towards 9 'pins', of which you have to knock as many as you can down. Also the village has a small garage which sells petrol and also hires out buses for school outings. Worton is very beautiful to look at and has a population of only 350 people so it is not totally ruined by overpopulation.

From a bird's eye view my estate looks like a double-headed snake winding its sinuous body in and out of the houses. The whole village, from a bird's eye view, looks like a tree spreading its branches to the outside world.

I would like to carry on living in Wiltshire because I don't like the busy industrial areas of places like London and I like the clean open air of the countryside.

I live in a small village called Edington on a farm, which my ancestors have lived on for 500 years. There are two parts to Edington. One part used to be called Tinhead and the other part Edington, but now the whole village is called Edington. The two parts are joined by council houses. Edington has a church that used to be a priory.

I am now going to tell you all about the people that live in Edington. There are quite a few old people who have lived all their life in Edington. One of these people is my grandfather who is 82. He said that his father had farmed here all his life and he wanted to carry on the farm after him. I also asked another person and she said that she was born here and her husband worked on a farm in the village and they liked staying around their family. This village does not have all old people living here. New people are moving in. These new people work in offices etc. in the nearby towns as Edington does not have very much employment.

Edington has changed a lot in the last thirty years. There used to be four pubs but gradually they were sold and made into private houses and now there is only one pub left. There was a bakery but this was sold as a private house too. There used to be a Post Office, but as the owners could not cope with the shop another person took it on in their garage. Recently the school (which had 21 pupils) was closed down. It has now been converted into a nursery school and an after school club.

One of the tourist attractions is the church. Every year there is a music festival held here which is when choirs from different churches come and sing and then people come and listen to them. Some of the services are broadcast on the radio. I ring the church bells for Sunday services. This might sound boring but is actually good fun and enjoyable. It is also good because I meet a lot of people and make friends.

I enjoy living in Edington. It is quiet and peaceful. I prefer living here than living anywhere else in the world.

I am a prodigal villager. Born, in a south Wiltshire village, at the end of the Second World War, in early adulthood I moved to the local town and returned, in my early fifties, to village life in mid-Wiltshire. The two villages of my experience have much in common: school, shop, post office, two churches, pub, builder's yard, village hall, farms, local bus service; but the ambience has totally changed in the years that I have been away.

I was born into farming and this remained my occupation until I wed, in my mid-twenties, when economic considerations led me to seek alternative employment. Throughout my first twenty-five years, village life was centred on the farming community. There were approximately six village farms, all run by local, working farmers, and all the farmyards and farmhouses were located within the village boundary. The farms themselves were not large, by today's standards, ranging in size from, approximately, seventy-five to three hundred acres, and were normally rented or, when owned, heavily mortgaged.

All of the other village businesses and facilities derived their income from the local farmers and farm workers. Thus farms were the economic engine of the village although, before I left, the role of the village was starting to change, as a few commuters were gradually moving in, whose income was derived from employment in the local town, seven miles away. However these newcomers were in the minority and were readily absorbed into village community life. This 'village life' truly did exist; everybody knew everybody else (and most of each other's business).

Travel was fairly limited. Most people walked, or cycled, to work and the majority, vehicular, village traffic was farm tractors which were so few that they could be individually identified by the sound of their engines. Working horses were a rarity and recreational horses non-existent. There was a daily bus service, providing two (early morning and late afternoon) week-day, round trips to the local town. There was also a weekly carrier service, for goods transport, which individuals on the route indicated their wish to use by hanging a white flag on their hedge.

Most village people purchased their routine provisions at the local shop, although some specialist items (e.g. paraffin oil) were supplied on a 'fortnightly round' basis. There was a strong urge for self-sufficiency, gardens being used to cultivate vegetables, rather than flowers, and allotments being provided and well used. Village people 'dressed up' to go to town, rarely ventured more than ten miles from home and residents of surrounding villages (two or three miles away) were viewed, with suspicion, as foreigners.

The village in which I now live is not centred on considerations of, or employment provided by, local farms, as most residents commute daily, or weekly, to their place of employment. The distances people commute is now much greater than previously considered practical, fifty miles or more being common. In fact the local town (seven miles away) is now itself a commuter town for many residents, who are employed in its much larger neighbour, twenty-five miles away.

The village pub, in common with many others, is not a meeting place for residents to swap local gossip, but an 'eaterie' attracting custom from a wide area. The village shop is principally a provider of specialist goods and services since most villagers travel to nearby supermarkets for their main, weekly household shopping. The village primary school is not merely for tuition of the local village children but derives many of its pupils from surrounding villages, who thus commence commuting long before they commence work. There are few local farms, but there are numerous local fields, owned by the more affluent villagers (who use them as paddocks for their horses) and, consequently, horses are a regular feature of village traffic.

In general, village residents' attitude to the countryside is totally altered, having previously been based on realism and economic necessity whereas now it is based on romanticism and reliance on food supplies from the local supermarket. The majority of village residents have no understanding of traditional country matters and little time, because of their work and travel commitments, to participate in village life. In the past villagers truly lived, and worked, in their village; nowadays they sleep, and sometimes play, in it.

I am Caroline Pile, aged 11 years and 5 months. I have a sister called Camilla. My mum is called Vanessa and my dad is called Malcolm. We live in a small hamlet called Lopcombe Corner. My five friends are called Emily Julian, Lyndsay Hutchings, Vicky Douglas, Emilia Page and Charlotte Lloyd-Williams. I have a few other friends but I don't keep in touch with them very well.

My father is a livestock farmer. He rears cattle and then sends them to market. *Is farming becoming extinct?* Cattle are getting harder to find and are being sold at £1.00 or less. Can you believe that a calf got sold for 80p, that's less than a hamster? They used to go for £50 or more each.

In Wiltshire the countryside is wonderful — you don't need to drive very much before you can see horses, cattle, sheep and even donkeys grazing. My five friends all live quite far away. I would like there to be a local footpath that is safe and far from the main road. The footpath should be connecting, eg Firsdown and Lopcombe Corner.

There are many clubs going on in Winterslow for example, Guides, rounders, Scouts, Cubs and so on. The clubs are well organised and plan good outings.

The school is great, it has its own swimming pool and will soon be producing its own sculpture garden for the year 2000 but I won't be there to see the finished product because I will be going to secondary school.

Hi, my name is Samantha, I was born in 1988 at Trowbridge Hospital and brought up in Westwood, near Bradford on Avon. I have just had my eleventh birthday. It was great fun, maybe even the best day of my life, so far! But there again I've had lots of good days and lots of fun days too.

But some days can be a disaster, like when I was six my Mum and Dad broke up. I hated that. Now my Mum lives in Trowbridge and I spend most of my time with her. I like to walk into Town at the weekends and go to the bookshop, I love reading.

In 1991 my sister Sarah came into my life. One of her worst days was when she developed asthma and had to be sent to hospital, she was very frightened at the time, but now she copes with it quite well. Yuck. I hate hospitals it makes me shudder to think about them.

We used to have two cats, a black one called Jinks and a white one called Lucky. Poor Jinks only had one eye. When I was eight he sadly died, that was in 1996. Everyone still remembers him, especially Lucky. They were great friends, probably the only friends Lucky's ever had. Lucky has great big yellow eyes, he's getting quite old now and doesn't move round much either. At Mum's we also have a cat, his name is Moorcroft, he's grey and very playful, he's just the cutest thing you ever saw.

I like going for walks in the countryside and having picnics on nice warm days, and best of all I like it when we have a bar-be-que in the garden and we chase around the garden with the hosepipe. We get absolutely soaked. I also like it in the winter when it snows, but that doesn't happen very often. It's also fun to fly the kite up on Westbury White Horse on windy days, we can see the horse from Mum's bedroom window, it always looks grey when it's about to rain. Sarah and I also enjoy riding our bikes along the towpath and through the woods.

Every morning at nine o'clock school starts. I have a lot of friends most of them I've known all my life. They are really good friends that are kind and caring. I try my very best to be the same, but sometimes it all goes terribly wrong!

Wiltshire. The downland, rolling and stretching to Salisbury Plain; the silence and mystery locked into the ancient landscapes of Avebury and Stonehenge; the thatched cottages nestling in villages, monuments to the slow but harder life of my ancestors.

Today, as the new millennium approaches, life is so different. During the week I live and work in the bustling town of (hoping to be a city) Swindon, but at weekends I escape and take long walks in our beautiful Wiltshire countryside. A Sunday for me is sheer heaven – driving to a country pub, tackling a circular walk of about five miles before returning to the pub for Sunday Roast, home for a hot bath, and later visiting the family or watching television.

Living at Stratton, Liddington Hill can be clearly seen from whichever direction I travel home – passing over Greenbridge; driving along the M4 coming from the east or the west; when travelling back from the seaside in the south; or from the Cotswolds in the north.

There is no doubt, Liddington is my beacon, reassuring me that I will soon be home. I watch the changing colours of the seasons over its form, conjuring magical memories of my childhood when, as the 'Dixon Street Gang', we would ride up there on our bikes and sit under the tall trees which bent and whistled in the cool wind.

Today, my Stratton home of more than thirty years is a haven tucked into a corner of a small cul de sac. The eighteen house community has a village atmosphere and many of our neighbours have lived here since the houses were built in 1959. We were parents of a young family in the 60s and our children still had some measure of freedom to roam, but the roads have become clogged with traffic. When driving to work now, I cross the newly constructed railway bridge at South Marston giving access to the yet-to-be-built rail-link yard, which will supposedly remove a lot of lorries from our roads. The new bridge is a far cry from the quiet, narrow bridge built by Brunel for horses and carts, which I crossed on the first day of my new job at the old Vickers factory more than fifteen years ago.

I want to preserve the peace and beauty of our downland but, at the same time, I want the convenience and comfort of getting to it. I want to drive to my job and the supermarket – Swindonians also need the new hospital being built in the fields at the foot of Liddington.

I hope that the way we travel will change, so that the beautiful downland of Wiltshire is not lost forever, after being protected by so many generations for me to enjoy. I would hope my grandchildren and their children will still be able to wonder at the peaceful waving wheat dotted with scarlet poppies, moving and sounding as if it were the sea flowing over this beautiful downland of my birth.

Mary E Powell

Burbage has seen many changes since I came here when I married John in 1957. Having lived in Burbage all his life John became sub-postmaster in 1959, when we built the present post office and house, and until our retirement in 1992 we were both very much involved in the business. At that time everyone knew everyone and families had lived in the same cottages for generations. From the mid-sixties with the development of Well Meadow, followed by the bungalows in East Sand, Burbage expanded rapidly. Three new developments took place from the early 1970s. With the building of Downlands, Burbage became a favourite home for retiring service personnel together with many young families who knitted well into the community. It was our privilege to know many so well.

In the late fifties, many jobs involved work on farms or the Great Western Railway. Today, several small businesses are run from home, and many commute to work in towns as far away as Bristol, London and beyond. The building of the bypass which was opened in 1991, was a wonderful achievement especially to those of us who fought so hard for it, and many will remember the night prior to its opening, and the Bypass Walk!

All Saints' Church of course plays an active part in our community, and its services attract worshippers from beyond the village. The Methodist Chapel closed in 1996 and is now being made into a home and successfully run business. Our primary school which was opened in 1989 replaces the old school in Eastcourt. It flourishes, and has 163 pupils (July 1999). The school is however in great need of extra classrooms. Pre-school children attend toddlers and playgroup which enable them to accept primary school easier. We are fortunate in having our own surgery run by Dr. Trevor King with the help of his wife Dr. Lucy. Various clinics held there save patients costly journeys further afield.

There are several organisations to suit all age groups, although some are not now so popular, nor can find leaders so easily as in the past. At the turn of this century, there were several public houses, shops and bakeries, many of which are now closed, and made into private houses. Coming up to the millennium, we are left with the White Hart and Three Horse Shoes public houses, our Post Office, where five postmen are fully employed too, East Sands Stores and newsagent, a D.I.Y. store and Hillside Garage which also sells groceries. Many village people now shop at supermarkets in nearby towns. Sadly to me, transport will never be the same with the closure under Beeching in the early sixties of Savernake Railway Station, Savernake High Level and Burbage and Grafton Stations, although inter-city trains still rush through the northern edge of the Parish. A more efficient bus service now serves the village, the Wigglybus having just been introduced, which hopefully will be popular. Burbage has three halls – the village hall, church hall and scout hall, all badly needing renovation; grants and lottery monies are being sought to update them.

From the early sixties John has been a member of the Parish Council, and for a number of years I acted as their clerk. Family and business commitments made me give this up eventually, much as I enjoyed the interest, which I still maintain through John.

Since our retirement in 1992, and having built our new home in our old garden, we are fortunate in having reasonably good health, and much enjoy life. John's involvement with Parish Council, now as their Chairman, mine with the Good Companions' Club (over 60s) of which membership is over a hundred, together with our interests in gardening, the Kennet and Avon Canal, where we use our narrowboat, walking and cycling (Savernake Forest and the Downs our favourite places) we find little time to spare.

Diane Poynting

On August 1st 1970, at the age of 23, I became a Welfare Assistant to the Child Care Officers based in the Old Fire Station, Salt Lane, Salisbury. I was the first Assistant in Wiltshire, but others quickly followed. Our accommodation was shared with the Welfare and Mental Health Departments and the Weights and Measures. The old fire siren was still in use and frequently brought an abrupt end to telephone conversations.

I was supplied with a brand new Austin Mini from the WCC Depot at Melksham, and regularly clocked up 2000 miles per month. I collected children from children's homes, police stations, foster homes etc.; sometimes I was accompanied by a Child Care Officer, but usually I was on my own. I regularly went alone on the fifty-mile run from Guildhall Courts to Langport Remand Home with three teenage boys in the car, and there were never any problems.

Another job was to collect babies, two or three days old, from Odstock Hospital and deliver them to foster homes to await adoption. The carrycot would simply be placed on the back seat of the Mini (there were no seat belts in those days). Sometimes my mother-in-law came to keep me company.

An occasion I remember well was going all the way to Southend Police Station, with a Child Care Officer in her Morris Minor, to collect a girl who had run away from a children's home. The local police did not even offer us a cup of tea, so we went to a café for a drink before collecting her and returning to Salisbury. The following day we took her to a secure home in Bristol. I also remember taking a pregnant girl to marry her boyfriend who was serving a sentence in Winchester Prison. I was a witness at the wedding.

The first Christmas after I joined the Children's Department, on the morning of Christmas Day, my husband and I took a bicycle to a boy who lived with his mother on Bemerton Heath. Every year the Department distributed toys, bikes etc. which had been restored by firemen at Boscombe Down in their rest periods.

When the Seebohm Report was implemented in 1973, the various branches of the Social Services were combined, and I began to work with elderly and disabled people as well as children. My job title became Social Work Assistant. In 1993 the departments were separated again, and I became part of the Adult Care Team. The lad we took the bike to is now 40, but I have visited his mum in my present post. The major part of my work is helping elderly people find places in residential and nursing homes, and arranging respite and home care for them

Would I go back to working with children? Things seemed simpler then, but financial restrictions and increased paper work have affected all social work. I find working with the elderly very rewarding and I think I'll stick with them.

Kirstie Priestley, age 13

I have lived in Wiltshire for most of my life. It strikes me, as I walk around Salisbury, and sometimes even Devizes, just how many tourists there are. I don't have very strong objections to tourists, apart from when they get in the way when you are trying to get on with your everyday life.

I often wonder why people come to Wiltshire. There are plenty of other counties with attractions. On the other hand, in Wiltshire there is Stonehenge, which not only looks impressive, it is also amazing to think how people carried the stones there over five thousand years ago. Avebury, just as impressive as Stonehenge, has fewer tourists visiting it. Although at both monuments, lots of stones have been removed, people still like coming to see them.

Salisbury, the only place in Wiltshire with a cathedral, also attracts large numbers of tourists. It is built on a water meadow and has the tallest spire in England. Some of its attractions are the oldest working clock in England, one of the four Magna Carta manuscripts and the cathedral's history. Americans in particular come to look at our monuments, as they have so little ancient history of their own.

The crop circle phenomenon has attracted large numbers of people to Wiltshire. Some are research scientists, trying to understand how the crop circles are formed. Others camp out on hillsides waiting to see a crop circle being made. Some of the people who come to see them go into the fields, ruin crops and make themselves unpopular with the farmers who own the fields.

Tourists can cause disturbance, but can also be good for an area. They provide jobs for people, working at the places they visit. People, generally, want souvenirs of the places they have visited, so local shops get additional business. If you compare all the good points with the bad ones you realise that they just about balance each other out. There are still lots of parts of Wiltshire which remain unspoilt and have not been invaded by tourists.

Jack Privet, age 11

● ●

I like grassy slopes. Swindon is good for bowling! Cinemas, Pizza Hut and food shops. Swindon is the largest Wiltshire town and it's still growing. They're building a new hospital near the M4 in Swindon. It should last for years.

Bruce Purvis

It used to be said that Birmingham, where I began my life as a librarian, was 'the city of a thousand trades'. Whilst Salisbury would be hard-pressed to boast as many, I should be surprised if, acre for acre, it is not as diverse in the activities of its people, now as in the past. My work as Salisbury's Local Studies Librarian reminds me constantly of the trades carried on in the City. I cannot walk from New Canal into Catherine Street without thinking of John Sidney Rambridge, jeweller, starting out in the Canal and taking over the premises of his old employer, James J. Gater, who remained next door for some years before moving to Catherine Street to succeed (and subsume) the old-established business of John Rumbold. Rambridge, like another jeweller in Catherine Street, James Macklin, was to serve Salisbury as its Mayor, and both their names are preserved as street names. Meanwhile, in Minster Street, Carters, established in 1817 is still going strong. (Until recently there was in their window a sapphire ring priced at £15000. The window is still intact, so someone must have bought it).

The very names of the streets suggest this bustle, with all the different trades and produce being plied, if not within the streets themselves, then within sight thereof. Until recently there were three butchers in Butcher Row: Pritchards survives nearby, a haven of properly prepared meat, in Fish Row, while in the Market Place, only a few yards from the Poultry Cross, Longleys of Wood Farm ('There are turkeys, and there are *Longley's* Turkeys') offer their own poultry, local dairy produce, game and Wiltshire bacon of unfailing quality on market days. Now that, with my wife working full-time, I share the food shopping, I am lucky to have a decent butcher, poulterer and greengrocer (in Crouch's of Butcher Row, or on the market) on hand.

On Fisherton Street, there is a huge variety of shops and trades, from *objets d'art* at the Fisherton Mill, to spares for domestic appliances (*serious* spares, like electric motors for washing machines, not just Hoover bags), to stamps at Dauwalder's to nearly-new clothes at Chain Reaction. Dauwalder's have given me valuable help with exhibition items, while at

Chain Reaction I bought my pride and joy among ties, a gold paisley, silk, from Gieves and Hawkes, for £14 – the most I have ever paid for a tie, but it was alleged to have retailed at £60. A little further down, Teed Tools has a range of tools, nuts, bolts, bits and pieces unmatched by any high-street trader within 20 miles, though the two market traders in tools have a fascinating collection of metalworking and light engineering tools.

My two favourite shops are in the curiously-named Endless Street. Above Sutton's at No. 3 is The Collector's Room – for collectors of recorded music, from which Edward Dowdell and his staff, Beryl, Matthew and John dispense new and second-hand CDs, LPs, wisdom and good humour in equal measure. The bulk of my music collection has come from The Room, and at a fraction of the new purchase price. A little further along is John Perkins who has traded in car spares and accessories from his little shop for over thirty years. With the advent of new technology in the motor trade and the music business as in my own career, I wonder for how far into the new millennium Edward, John and I will still be here: I am sure we shall be, but our lives will not be as they are today.

Rowena Quantrill

I've spent much of my life moving around the world and when my husband retired from the Diplomatic Service in 1994 we settled in Bradford on Avon. I loved this beautiful and friendly town immediately though I found I missed the travel and the friendship of people of a diversity of races and cultures: Wiltshire generally is a very 'white' county. To compensate, however, there are plenty of folk here who have travelled and lived overseas or simply keep up a keen interest in other countries. At the Africa Connection group we meet people who have lived in Africa, some for much of their lives, and through the local Oxfam Group I can campaign on behalf of people in developing countries. I have also been drawn into groups such as Wiltshire Agenda 21 when they organise events like Wiltshire Fair Trade Fortnight.

One thing I soon discovered on moving here was the demands on the time of the 'active retired'. With a view that one day we might need the service ourselves, my husband and I joined the Bradford on Avon Link Scheme in its fledgling days. Part of a chain of Wiltshire Links, Bradford Link concentrates mainly on driving elderly people to medical appointments, shopping etc. I have seen the scheme expand rapidly and been shocked by the need which has been uncovered. Part of our reason for moving to Bradford was to be near my mother, and I have been glad to be close enough to support her through the onset of Parkinson's disease and crippling arthritis. Many old people in Wiltshire, however, have no close relatives living near and are battling alone with their daily routine. Some feel they cannot cope any more and are forced into the agonising decision to move into a nursing home by their physical frailty though being still fully alert mentally.

One aspect of our lifestyle in retirement, which I had in no way foreseen, was the way we have come to be dominated by the computer. Once we had an e-mail address I was hooked. I have always loved communicating and networking and what better way to do it than by e-mail. Messages flow back and forth with old friends from many stages of our life. Our daughter travelled for a year but we were never left wondering how she was as she went from cyber café to cyber café sending reassuring notes. Our son took part in hang-gliding competitions in Europe and I tapped in to the Hang-gliding Association web site each day to follow his progress.

Now we are a two computer family for my husband got fed up with the hours of computer time I was taking up and suggested I get my own. Just as well, as I am now using it to edit the newsletter of the Wiltshire Ornithological Society, Oh yes... birds. Now there's another hobby. My life in Wiltshire is never dull.

Janet Repton

We first came to Bradford on Avon in 1966 during a visit to Bristol and Bath. It was love at first sight, later to be consummated when, out of three weavers' cottages advertised in *The Times*, we bought 31 Tory. The views were superb, but water trickled down the inner rockface walls! However, we had a roof, which was more than could be said for some of our neighbours and most of Middle Rank. For twenty-one years the house gave us tremendous pleasure, rest and relaxation from teaching in Inner London comprehensive schools. From our London flat, just behind the BBC, we travelled by Underground to Paddington on Friday evenings. We could either sleep or read on the train. The double-decker bus from Bath would wheeze up Winsley Hill and soon we were gazing at the White Horse. Bliss!

The house cost £1,750 plus £850 to repair – a small fortune to us then. Mortgages were difficult to obtain, but Mr. Hillier, at that time the only estate agent, got one for us. We paid £20 per month, a large sum in 1967.

In 1981 my husband retired and, as the school population in Central London was declining, I was, luckily, able to take early retirement, so we both left central London to live permanently in Wiltshire. We became involved with duscussions at County Hall when the Green Belt was drawn up around the town. In 1983 I campaigned to prevent the rail line being singled between Bath and Trowbridge. More recently, with the privatisation of British Rial, I campaigned to keep the computer for through ticketing in our station booking office.

Sadly, in 1987 my husband became ill and we had to leave Tory a year before he died. We sold 31 Tory for £45,750. It was sold before it was advertised. For some time my life lacked any real meaning, but in 1991 I was asked to stand as a Liberal Democratic Town and District Councillor. To my amazement and joy, I was elected. I had some training with the Citizens Advice Bureau and this proved valuable. Being a councillor is interesting and worthwhile work. Helping others and endeavouring to keep Bradford a thriving and attractive town is very satisfying. The building I now live in belonged to the Methuen family in the 1690s. From my kitchen window I can see 31 Tory. It was recently sold to a young couple for £100,000. May they be as happy as we were!

● ●

The rumble of the Cub Scouts meeting in the main hall can be heard by everyone, except Major Baker. Shiny folding tables are extracted from a morass of Playgroup toys under the stage, the uncomfortable orange plastic chairs are arranged, and the meeting comes to order.

'Apologies?' Mrs Ryde, by gender outnumbered one to four, is in the chair. There is sympathy for Mr Caxton, 71, absent, recuperating from a long visit from his three grandchildren. Less sympathy is shown for the County Councillor, a stalwart supporter of parish council causes, but absent through pressure of business village affairs which come before County Hall here.

'Cooptions?' Vacancies are slow to fill. Parish councillors need to be hard working, caring, with thick skins, local knowledge, endurance and the ability to read quickly a monthly mound of circulars updating them on matters ranging from dog fouling to visiting arts groups.

'Minutes of the previous Meeting. Amendments?' Enthusiasm manifests itself – just. The clerk is a retired schoolmaster and a townie; it is gratifying to catch him out on some error of syntax or fact.

'Matters Arising?' The floodgates open. The chairman, she insists on the title, strives to keep the flow in separate, manageable channels. The Major, disadvantaged by hearing years of gunfire on the Plain, dodges from one item to another. There has been more vandalism at the playground and broken bottles have been found under the slide. The County Council have at last installed the long promised street light – in wrong place. (It shines brilliantly into the Chairman's bedroom but does not illuminate the dark path, often booby trapped with horse manure from the riding school).

'Agenda Item 5. Bus Shelter.' They know about national and county efforts being made to promote public transport, but have a dilemma. The bus company threaten to reduce their service, passengers get fewer all the time. The clerk explains that he can get grant aid from three sources for bus shelters. "Reading the guff you could probably have one each – only one-sixth of their cost falling on the parish council. With a little imagination we might even make a profit." The clerk has a long running squabble with the District Auditor so his last remark is ignored; he certainly won't record it.

'Planning.' Their local knowledge and good sense make for useful contributions towards these matters. NIMBYism is rarely allowed rein. It is a pity the District Council are so often cavalier about their opinions, and their efforts at enforcement invariably a source of merriment or dismay. "When does a mobile home become a dwelling under the Agricultural Labourers Act 1923?"

'Accounts.' The clerk produces copies for all. This is a time for detail. They and their parishioners pay. Payments are passed for the old man who tidies the graveyard; the instalment on the mortgage for the parish hall – four figures; replacement Neighbourhood Watch signs (£10 each) and the clerk's salary and expenses. "You use a lot of envelopes Fred?" Questions are asked about the donation towards the Substances Abuse Foundation but £100 is voted. They have a shrewd idea about the trouble in the playground. Finally they pay the Youth Club £200 towards their sports kit.

'Any Other Business' is the usual disaster area, and the Chairman mutters darkly about business being done better with proper notice – but AOB persists.

It's like Parish Councils... enduring... and important.

Margaret Roberts

My husband and I were moved to North Wiltshire 33 years ago by his employer Westinghouse. We decided to settle in Hullavington as it was between Chippenham and Malmesbury, close to the new motorway which was about to be built and there were only a few modern properties.

At that time there were five farms working off the main street, two with milking herds and the high spot of the day was to watch the cows going along The Street to and from the milking parlours. Sometimes both herds were out at the same time. The passage of time has seen two farms relocate to the outskirts of the village while two others shut down completely. The farmyards are now covered with Executive style housing and cows are rarely seen. Also in 1966 there were two shops, Post Office and garage. Now the garage houses the only shop and Post Office.

In 1971, after eleven years of fund-raising by villagers from Bingo, Jumble Sales, Raffles, etc. a new Village Hall was built and this went a long way to integrating the 'newcomers' into village life. At this time the number born and raised in the village was still larger than newcomers, but we all worked and played together starting up the Playgroup, Drama Group (which had been 'resting' for a few years), Over Sixties and forming an organisation to run Entertainments for all. This involved dances with live music, parties for the children at Christmas, four-day trips to Holland and Jersey and organising an annual Carnival.

This latter event ran for twelve years and involved the whole village in various activities throughout the week, culminating in a procession of floats through the village led by a brass band and majorettes, followed by a fête either at the school or on the village green. The best carnival was held in 1984 but the annual fête is still held on the first Saturday in July, now run jointly by the school parents, staff and members of the village hall committee. It is the second fête of the summer, the first being run by the Church early in June. Each event raised approximately £1,000 in 1999 and was well attended.

Since 1987 I have worked as Administration Officer at the village primary school, mornings only. At that time we had 78 children on roll in four classes, nearly half coming from RAF families. When we return for the Autumn Term 1999 there will be approximately 160 children in six classes with 52% from Service families from a Supply Regiment RLC which took over the camp in 1990. Of course, in 1987 there was no computer in the office, Local Management of Schools, National Curriculum, Literacy or Numeracy hours.

So as the millennium closes Hullavington has doubled in size in forty years and residents no longer work within ten miles, instead a large proportion commute to Swindon, Bristol and beyond, but the community spirit is still alive!

Robin Elizabeth Robson

Perhaps it was the pond, or the pub that looked so pretty, leaning on the village green. Or perhaps it was the house that felt just right. Either way, on that March day in 1976, we decided that our new home would be in Biddestone in Wiltshire. We are not native to the south of England; the much loved home we left was in Northumberland, that unknown and majestic most northerly county.

The past year or two have seen big changes in our village. We lost our village shop – it was burgled, and as it is at the top of a cul de sac, and nobody heard anything, it was unnerving. Fortunately only money was stolen, nobody was threatened or hurt, but confidence was lost. Now we have lost that most valuable of places, with the best postmistress ever, a place to meet, and commodities to purchase.

The village school closed last July; there just were not enough children to make it 'economically viable', that awful expression. Our children are now bussed to the area school at Yatton Keynell, to the aptly name 'By Brook School'. Where the mothers used to congregate, just by Elm House, waiting for the children to come out of school, they now wait for the bus. Still time to count the ducklings, watch the colour of the water, see if there is a fish, wonder where the Canadian Geese have come from, or where they have gone to. Earlier this year, to everyone's surprise, a beautiful swan arrived, it did not stay long, but we loved its visit. The children are kind, they do not chase the ducks or throw things at them, only food. Some visitors allow their offspring too much freedom by the pond, and they frighten the birds.

St. Nicholas is a Saxon-Norman Church, so very old. It has been extended and extended; though it is still small. When it is absolutely full, it only takes 120 people. There is a large congregation for such a small village, and services are held twice on a Sunday and on a Wednesday morning. It is easy to feel close to God in this beautiful place. We added a kitchen and a loo last year, and later this year Bishop Barry is coming from Bristol to open it officially. It is the only meeting place that we have, other than the two pubs. We have never had a Village Hall, though we are fundraising like mad to try and build one in conjunction with the Sports Club.

The village mix is changing. Because the houses sell for a premium, young people, raised in the village, are unable to afford to buy them and we are getting people who only spend weekends here. So sad.

One old lady once grumbled that you are not allowed to get old in Biddestone, there just is not enough time. There is always someone to see and people to care.

Kate Ryan, age 10

Who am I? Today I am Kate Ryan, aged 10, of Winterslow CE Primary school. Tomorrow? Who knows?

My life is not extraordinary. I am part of a family of six. Mum, Dad, Lucy (nine), James (six) and Thomas (four). We also have a dog. My dad has to drive a long way to work so I do not see him as often as my mum.

I do not have a best friend . I have a lot of people who I know and like. People are all very friendly so it is hard to choose between them.

I have not always lived in Wiltshire. It is at first glance a beautiful although habit-based place. But if you look just a bit closer you will find it is a big, big community of people. Nothing bad happens all the time. When it does it is usually on the front page of the Salisbury Journal, which is mostly achievements and decisions.

Although I like Wiltshire I still think there is room for improvement! For instance the bus services could be on time, and the swimming pool is not up to scratch.

Another little concern I have with Wiltshire is that there is not a beach anywhere in the county. You have to travel a long way in a car to reach a beach. Still there are plenty of rivers. However I enjoy all the shops in Salisbury and like the historical side of things.

All in all Wiltshire is a nice place with good facilities (you can often see me at the library) and mostly friendly people. It isn't a bad place to live and you would have to look hard to find a much better one.

Of course now Wiltshire might be ruined by modernisation. The wildlife might have turned into fossils. Buses might have disappeared completely. All I can tell you is what life is like in Wiltshire in the year 1999 for an ordinary ten year-old school girl.

Janet Rymer

Is it being an indigenous resident of Amesbury, born in the war, but now living in a far more transient environment, that makes me sometimes ponder on things that seem solid and unchanging? Cars have replaced bicycles; shops have replaced thatched cottages; a night club has replaced a dance hall and a huge influx of military personnel has ensured that the accent of 'the moonraker' is the exception rather than the rule.

Amongst this faster and noisier life, bells still ring out from a church whose foundations date back to 979. Climbing the forty-eight steps to ring the bells, I often wonder about the countless generations who've trodden the same path. Did they go on a two year campaign to have their bells repaired? Probably not. Maybe the church was then rich enough, or perhaps the landed gentry would have footed the bill. But even such a timeless art as bellringing is open to change.

With the millennium approaching and bells very much a part of the celebrations, it was realised that Amesbury's bells were in dire need of attention. Estimates were obtained. What a shock! Someone would have to find £35,000 before the year 2000. But who? If we could show that someone would find £17,500 lottery funding may pay the other half. In anticipation of a near miracle a grant was applied for.

Hurrah for a diverse set of talents! With a tower captain who's given the bells nearly fifty years of tender loving care, a bellringer who filled forms designed to deter the fainthearted, and a team of determined 'mature' ladies who became adept regulars at car boot sales selling jam and cakes, fundraising took off.

Well! If anyone thinks that community spirit is stone dead in the last part of the twentieth century, think again. As the word spread, local organisations and individuals, unfortunately too numerous to mention, ensured that the coffer swelled and in March we obtained a millennium grant. In the nick of time we reached our target.

On I5th June I999 the eight bells were lowered forty feet from the tower to the church floor, as of old, by sheer manpower and a set of pulleys. As the eighth and heaviest bell, weighing 22 cwt. completed the operation, a team of bellringers and volunteers emerged from the door, smiling, dirty and undoubtedly several pounds lighter.

Having got nearly six tons of bells outside the church door, it was found that the lorry that was to transport them to Bridport for repairs was too large for the church drive. All was not lost. Our mayor, farmer Crook, arrived with his fork lift truck. Usually booted, hatted and belted, he added his mayoral chain for such an historic occasion.

Amesbury's bells *will* ring out for the millennium, thanks to many without the accent of a 'moonraker'. They're justly called 'our community.'

R.M. Salt

I had flown gliders, aeroplanes, helicopters and airships over a period of 43 years. What might I have flown a hundred years hence?

The day started, as usual, just before 6.30am. A shower now, or a bath later? Opting for the bath, downstairs to an enthusiastic welcome from the dogs, two chocolate labrador bitches, mother and daughter. The TV beamed business news interspersed with local news, sport and the weather forecast: the forecast is generally accurate except for the timing – a function of our being an island. Breakfast is unhurried: unusually porridge is cooked overnight in the Aga's slow oven; herb tea upstairs for the lady of the house still horizontal for another hour or so.

No more than ten yards (metres if you are young) from the house, the start of beautiful safe walks for the dogs. First, unlock the church: surprising how many visitors appear early in a churchyard – some just inquisitive, others to have a quiet moment in the church, others to find the grave of a relative. Our plan of the churchyard helps enormously there. A quick look around the church to check that the roof hasn't fallen in, and no obvious vandalism. Recently we lost to vandals the small brass cross from the top of a churchwarden's stave: a sad reflection of our times.

Our church is recorded to date back to the 800s and last month we have become aware of tangible evidence of a connection with our forbears' use of the church. As of habit I glance at the recently discovered pilgrims' crosses carved in stone in the east jamb of the church door, I ponder their (in-) significance compared with the distances and wonder of space.

We continue our walk beside the Wylye, noting the water level, clarity, weed growth, wildlife, and look especially for pike, which devastate the fish population and occasionally devour ducklings, young grebe and moorhens. The younger one sometimes brings to me a proudly acquired, always alive, pigeon or rat! Three miles later, our daily obligatory survey of the river completed, we are back at the house.

There is a list of household and gardening chores awaiting. A house 300 years old is always demanding attention. Not long ago, I found a token in the garden. It dated from 1540 –1550 and was used for gambling. But chores have to wait for our weekly shopping trip to Salisbury. Sadly the village shop and post office closed three years ago and a centre of gossip and information has been lost, probably forever.

The shopping done a second walk for the dogs and there is time to mow the lawn before preparing for one of five committee meetings this week. I cannot think of any 'true' villager on any of our village committees or councils. We have lived here for thirty years, longer than most residents, but we accept that we are still incomers! Their lack of representation on committees gives the villagers liberty and opportunity to point the finger when things go wrong or unpopular decisions are made. Never mind, it's all taken in good part, we all get on well together and good-humoured criticism does no-one any harm.

Rather late, I remember to lock the church and give the dogs their last, albeit shorter, walk. Too cloudy for star gazing tonight. Do you know that when you look at the Orion nebula, you are seeing it as it was in 1066?! Sleep well.

● ●

Here we go again, another day, another week. What lies ahead?

An 8.15 start on Sunday, off to the capital with the RBL Ladies to visit the Chelsea Pensioners Home. If on time, we will go to morning service in the chapel and so Lady Thatcher and her spouse are often there, that will be our touch of class for the week.

Monday. Autumn Club. This was an eye-opener for me, the first time I went it just happened to be a member's 70th birthday and before the usual cup of tea, we all had a sherry. There was orange juice for any abstainers but I didn't notice many! Next meeting, some routine – and the next – so it was a disappointment when on the fourth occasion the sherry well had run dry.

Tuesday. Another early start, why do hospitals give septuagenarians 9 a.m. appointments? In former days we would have welcomed them but were invariably given afternoon peak times, now with a thirteen-mile journey involved, we get this. Sod's law I suppose.

WI tonight and an easy competition. 'My most treasured possession'. For me it's a picture of my childhood home, the village shop in Lyneham. Painted before the days of Hercules, NAAFIs and Royal visits.

Wednesday. A quick dust round, nothing too strenuous, remember I am creeping towards my own particular century!

Bowling today so a couple of paracetamols will help me through the two hours at the Olympiad. Up and down those mats about thirty times plus all the bending does wonders for the waistline but the back protests.

Thursday. A friend comes for the day so a quick hoover to follow on from yesterday's dusting. Luckily the flat (one of 33 purpose-built for the over 60s) faces the garden and does not collect much dust. My mother would have loved it – she would not however have taken kindly to the fire alarm which goes off periodically for various reasons such as burning toast, flies on the smoke alarm etc.

I can well imagine what the firemen say after they have catapulted themselves down the pole and find "it's those flats again" but there is never a word of reproach.

Friday. Market day in town and the WI stall will be sold out if I am not there early. Free-range eggs, home-cooked bread and pies, yummy jams and pickles, it's all there.

Another bowling afternoon, thank goodness there is now a handrail for the steps outside the Olympiad, thanks to NWDC.

Lastly Saturday. A day to explore. A pub lunch with friends and a walk up the canal path at Seend – or Bradford-on-Avon. Or a trip to Keynes Water Park with a picnic, who knows?

What more can I tell you to prove that life in the late 20th century can be busy and interesting if you are lucky enough to be able to get around.

Gordon Sharp

We're a pretty varied lot here, mostly incomers these days, with only a few of the old village left. There were 488 of us at the last census, probably not many more than at the last Millennium, when our village was *Sumreford*, and held by Alfward from the Abbot.

No-one holds us now. There isn't a 'squire', and our public affairs are regulated by accommodation and compromise within a group of perhaps forty people. This group provides most members of our institutions, such as the Parish Council, Village Hall Committee, Parochial Church Council and WI Committee, attends most village functions, plays skittles, digs allotments and, I think, takes the most pleasure in our village and its pasture land setting. That doesn't mean we're a divided village. Not everyone has time or inclination for village matters, but they're welcome to join in when they have.

There are just two farms now, down from seven in the 1940s, and most of us work in nearby towns, or as far as Bristol and even London. There are RAF people, a geologist, builders, bankers, teachers, accountants, architects, the water-bailiff, auctioneers and financiers. We have a garage, a car repair business, a pub/restaurant, but no shop, post office or school – they all went during the 1980s and 90s There is a bus service, now better than it was, but you need a car to get around.

The fields and hedgerows of our parish are much the same now as they were on the tithe map of 1847. Rabbits and foxes abound, and deer are increasing. Buzzards have been back for several years. If anything, our environment is improving.

We have few burning issues as the Millennium approaches. Our 14th century church needs re-roofing, a ponderous process involving English Heritage, the Diocese and architects. The Village Hall, a classic World War One army hut, is to be extended, kitchened and looed, but should retain its period charm into another century. There are occasional planning flurries as in-fill houses are built, but planning policy appears to protect the village from major change or expansion. A Millennium village green is to be inaugurated on land left over from the last big expansion of the village, when some thirty houses were built on a field called Vale Leaze in the 1960s. There will also be a new Garden of Remembrance in the cemetery. Finally for this millennium, some of us are wondering if we can restore an 18th century hour-sounding mechanism for the church bells. Fine if you live several hundred yards away, maybe not so good for the neighbours – this could be a big issue!

Are we too comfortable? Would the young agree that there are few problems here? These are things I do not know. I only know that to be part of village life in late 20th Century England is a great pleasure and privilege. May it remain so.

Sarah Singleton

Willow trees grow above the Swallowhead spring where it flows into the River Kennet. Silbury Hill towers beyond the river. In the June evening sunshine, the silky blades of young wheat are a vivid, translucent green. It is Midsummer's Eve, and we have ribbons.

We walk across the soft earth, knobbly with flints, to the muddy dell where the bank falls away to the river. The waters from the spring meander through fierce nettles and succulent, fleshy grasses to the Kennet. The willows are already adorned. Strips of brightly coloured fabric decorate the lower branches, rippling and flicking in the breeze. Wicker rings dangle, and higher up, someone has fastened a set of tinkling chimes.

My six year-old daughter peers at the offerings at the spring. A hunk of quartz crystal, a dream catcher, a crude clay statuette of the Earth goddess, huge thighs and breasts, but headless.

"Can I have them?" she queries, stretching out a hand to plunder the shrine.

Then we realise we are not alone. Five people, clad in motley, step out from the trees. A girl plucks discordant notes on a mandolin. A young man, with thick, brown hair, greets us. We are all shy, but everyone smiles.

"We're in a band," the young man says, "the Spacegoats." He looks at me hopefully, but I haven't heard of them. We discuss the state of the river, which is lower than usual. He blames the water companies, for over-pumping. Then they sing a song, an odd, magical tune, echoing among the willows.

We tie up our ribbons. We make a wish. Then we head for the car park at Silbury Hill where numerous vans and tents are assembled. The sun declines. The tribes gather. Bikers, latter-day pagans, students, travellers. Two girls, their faces patterned and painted, skip past in a whirl of colour. We sleep fitfully, in a tent. Underfoot the bruised grass smells sharp and herby.

The sky clouds over so at dawn we don't see the sunrise. Instead the cloud pales, from black, to grey and oatmeal, to white. From the top of Silbury Hill a horn sounds. People cheer and ululate. Across the fields, we see the flash of flame as brands of fire are juggled atop West Kennet Long Barrow. A man with long grey hair celebrates a hand-fasting for a pale girl in a crown of ivy and a gawky young man in a green cloak. They kiss, and leap over a fire.

The longest day begins.

Paul Snook

Recently I left the hubbub and mayhem of the city for the supposed peace and tranquillity of the countryside. Or so I thought. Far from resembling a rural idyll; livestock gently lowing and locals leaning on gates watching nothing in particular, it is in fact a very noisy place. Allow me to explain.

I moved from St. Paul's in Bristol where there is perhaps a little bit more than your average hustle and bustle. Heavy traffic noise, sirens, screeching tyres, shouts, screams and laughter, it all rolls into one relentless aural onslaught. Yet we lived quite happily with this cacophony. We became inured to the din, so much so that we only noticed it when it was gone. No cars? No noise? Heads turn as people look around, curiously, trying to come to terms with this sudden lapse into silence. Then, like a metallic flash flood, the traffic reappears and normality resumes.

So how does this compare to serene and placid backwater Wiltshire? Well for a start it was very rare for our flat in St. Paul's to be shaken by the sound of heavy artillery. As we live directly below Salisbury Plain, and the Army has to practice, flinging its excess munitions around, this is a regular feature in our lives. St. Paul's also lacks something that exists here in great abundance, and that is lawns. Where there are lawns there are, of course, lawnmowers. Not like the little push-along of obscure vintage used by my father to massacre the patch of moss lovingly referred to as a lawn by him and with derision by the rest of us. No, I refer to machines that range from small self-propelled tanks through to behemoths that could happily mow an area the size of Texas.

Why are men (and it is invariably men) obsessed with mowing the lawn? Betwixt sunrise and sunset, seven days a week, the air is filled with the sound of petrol-driven grass butchery. Lawnmowers driven by men who deem themselves good neighbours, oblivious to the fact that there are people around them trying to grab a few moments of relaxation, away from the traffic jams and commuting minefield.

I may, just for experimental purposes you understand, start my motorcycle up at nine o'clock on a Sunday morning and leave it running for a couple of hours, purely to see how many complaints I receive. If I did exactly the same with a lawnmower I would just be the proud neighbour who's concerned that the grass has sprouted an extra millimetre overnight and is looking unsightly.

Please, for the sake of my sanity, give the grass a fighting chance and just sit on the lawn with a good book instead.

William Spray

On the north west edge of Marlborough and not to be confused with the differently shaped ecclesiastical parish, Preshute Parish is entirely within the North Wessex Area of Outstanding Natural Beauty, has a valued stretch of the River Kennet running through it, cannot boast a village, contains thousands more livestock than humans, has just three significant settlements each some three crow-flown miles from any of the others, and has had since 1973 a Parish Council which is the one formal link between them.

In acreage and variety of activity Temple Farming, Rockley, is the most significant of the three settlements. The name comes from the Knights Templar, the land being one of the many properties they developed in the twelfth and thirteenth centuries to support their activities in the Holy Land. What was once Temple Bottom Barn within their thirteenth century Temple Farm is now the hub of the largest farming enterprise in Wiltshire - 1719.23 hectares, 1,100 of them within the Parish; mixed farming, with a wide range of crops and an organic unit; a National Hunt Stud; a Point-to-Point course; venue for the revived annual Marlborough Cup and Country Fair, which this year attracted some 20,000 racegoers and families; woodlands and gallops and shooting; two machinery dealerships; and in it all – through the planting of native species woodlands, the miles of hedgerows restored or newly established, the restoration of dew ponds, the encouragement of endangered creatures such as owls – extensive contributions to biodiversity. Including Chris Musgrave, Estate Manager, there are, living on the estate and sharing in its work, 26 adults – Councillor Mrs Cowley among them – and, at present, six children.

By contrast, with 60 of its 75 employees and 25 spouses and children living there, Manton House Estate has easily the largest concentration of population in the Parish. The Estate covers some 2,200 acres and is devoted to racehorse-training and to farming – 1,000 acres to crops; 700 to grass pasture; and 100 acres of woodland and tracks. In addition to the crops the Manton House Farm Manager, Councillor John Lister, and seven other resident workers cope with 300 head of beef cattle and three bulls; 1,300 ewes which, aided by 32 rams, produce some 2,300 lambs each season. With Peter Chapple-Hyam as trainer for Robert Sangster since 1991, there have been as many as 120 horses in training this year, half of them owned by Swettenham Stud. Roughly equal numbers of two and three year-olds, with only a very few older horses, are all trained for the flat.

The third settlement, Clatford, has at its cross-roads the one Parish Council property – a small bus shelter – and the Parish noticeboard. With 660 acres for crops and sheep and beef cattle, Councillors Hugh and Ian Wroth are amongst those who farm in the vicinity; there is a small Stables enterprise; and so far, though with low-cost housing getting scarcer, there is a range of privately-owned dwellings unmatched in any other part of the Parish. It feels, because it is, a community with a stimulating mix of very different interests and backgrounds – Councillor Mrs Upton, hard-working owner of Marlborough's countrywear shop, and her falconer husband among them. It is also able to mobilise friendly effective campaigns for things like the bus shelter and for better road signs and markings. And then there is Elm Tree Farm whose buildings, adapted for light industrial use, now blend less happily, in appearance as in activities, into a rural environment.

The countryside quality of this AONB Parish will be maintained only by lively vigilance and by strong determination to be always as constructive, but above all as responsible, as possible over development that, either in direct assault or gradual erosion, could all too easily destroy for ever at least part of a heritage that is not ours to despoil.

Louise Starkey, age 10

I have a sister called Isabel, a mum called Jenny, a dad called David and a dog called Pollie.

On a school day, when I get up the first thing I do is get dressed. Then I go downstairs and have breakfast. For breakfast I will normally have a bowl of cereal (usually Branflakes or Weetabix) followed by a slice of toast. For a drink I will have pure orange juice. When upstairs again, I brush my teeth, wash my face and put on my shoes. My hair is brushed and by 8.20 a.m. hopefully — everyone should be in the car and reversing out of the gate.

At school, on different days of the week, we do different things. Here is a table that shows them.

Monday — Gym and a spelling test.
Tuesday — Tables test.
Wednesday — Swimming.
Thursday — Normal school work
Friday — Games.

There are clubs that go on after school run by the members of staff and outside of school. Here is a chart that tells you which clubs go on and which ones I do (outside of school):

DAY	CLUB	I DO/DON'T
Monday	Chess	X
Tuesday	Art	X
Wednesday	Choir	3
Thursday	Athletics	3
Friday	Recorder	3

On Mondays after school we take my sister to gym at Trowbridge Sports Centre and bring her home again. On Wednesdays after choir club both my sister and I go to ballet in Bradford. And on Saturday mornings I go to trampolining at Trowbridge Sports Centre.

On Sundays we normally have a lie-in. At about 9.00 a.m. everyone is having their breakfast and after that will get dressed. Then we will have quite a relaxing day. Either shopping in Bath or Bristol (sometimes Trowbridge), or a family outing or gardening/decorating the new house

In Wiltshire the countryside is lovely. We used to live in Westwood (three months ago) and now we live in Winsley. (Not very far away. Just down one side of the valley and up the other!)

On the way to school in the early spring, sometimes summer, we see lambs, calves, foals and lime-green rolling hills.

Winsley is quite a quiet place now that the bypass has been built and full of friendly people. The shop is close by and there's a church, social club and school as well. Everything you need!

I would definitely say that Wiltshire is a very handy but enjoyable place!

My Wiltshire day starts with the alarm clock at 5:30 am. This is so I have time for some rudimentary home keep-fit (sit-ups, exercise bike), take my wife tea in bed, shave, shower, breakfast and dress at a gentle pace, without having to rush. At 7:30 I set off for work 19 miles away in Swindon.

My job is computer engineer. Four years ago I was downsized (made redundant) from my post as IT manager for a large publishing company, and being over forty 1 was deemed too old to be re-employed. Self-employment was therefore the best option. For the past two years I've worked as a short-term contractor in tech support at Railtrack, which has its Great Western zone HQ in Swindon.

The department – about ten of us – maintain and troubleshoot a network of ten file servers and around 700 computer users spread over four main offices in Swindon with outbases at Bristol, Gloucester, Cardiff, Exeter and Reading, plus an assortment of signal boxes from Penzance to Birmingham, Port Talbot to the edge of London. Most of the work involves helping office staff to use their computers, fixing breakdowns, ministering to the needs of the systems like a shepherd watching his flock of sheep.

A lot of work these past few months has been geared to getting our systems ready for the millennium date change and to get safely through the perilous time of the Millennium Bug. 'Y2K' has been part of our communal IT lives for the past two or three years, but with the approach of The Day there is a gradual increase in the tension. Meetings, briefings, training for the event are building up. Software changes developed over the past year are being rolled out weekly.

On top of that the daily round of looking after the users goes on. Equipment failures or system 'glitches' - something doesn't work, then it does, for no apparent reason – and a lot of user ignorance. These things are supposed to be easy to use, but software is actually quite complex and users are rarely trained in its full complexity.

We're a close-knit working team, but mix little outside work. We live all over the zone, so there's more impetus to get home than to hang around. My homeward journey is a reversal of the morning workbound trip – join the traffic convoy, little opportunity to overtake and little reason to do so (gain three car lengths and get to the next traffic lights five seconds earlier). Once home it's an evening meal, then maybe more work (I keep my small business of internet web site design going) or, if it's a warm evening, maybe a stroll along the canal from Devizes to the Bridge at Horton and a drink in the pub garden. Sometimes it's television, but either we're more discerning than we once were, or there really is only rubbish on most of the time.

Trevor Storer

As dawn breaks, Mary Morris pedals her Post Office bike along Bourne View for the last time. During the hours of darkness, the Avonmore milkman has completed his doorstep deliveries disturbing the lighter sleepers in Wyndham Lane and consignments of bread, cakes and dry cleaning have been delivered to Rob and Sandra's general store.

As the mail arrives from Salisbury Sorting Office, Pete Smith is making his way to the Garage where he sorts out the newspapers as the first early morning customers arrive. Mike Brunton calls in en route to his publishing firm in Thruxton where the next edition of *Clayshooting* magazine is being prepared. Mike's son has just become the youngest world champion at the sport. Stuart Haslam who will be 15 years-old on lst January 2000 completes his paper round in the nick of time as pupils of Salisbury schools make their way wearily to the bus stop after another late night in the playground.

The village now boasts a new bus shelter after pressure on the Parish Council from this enterprising group. Commuters leave for work in the surrounding towns and the A338 becomes momentarily busy. As the traffic dies down the Idmiston school bus starts picking up its passengers, not as many as usual as some mums have travelled separately to the end of term service. Toddlers arrive at the Chapel for another session of the thriving playgroup and if the weather holds they will be able to cross the road into the recently refurbished playground.

The village falls quiet, the silence occasionally punctuated by delivery vans searching for unnumbered houses or planes aimlessly circling Boscombe Down. The library van arrives and is met by its regular literary group. By now some people are working at home. Rob Kitson is preparing an article for the *Guardian*, Dave Leech is working on security matters in anticipation of his next trip to China, the members of the Art Club are putting the final touches to their work for the annual exhibition, and Harry Lodge a member of the Amore E Vita (Love and Life) cycling team, supported by the Pope, heads off for more practice.

The fields around contain the usual crops – rape, wheat, barley, field beans and this year the set-aside has been adorned by the vivid yellow and purplish blue haze of sunflowers and phaseolus. At the Old Inn Yvonne and Roy prepare another day's hospitality reflecting on the pub's success in the Spire FM Quiz (semi-finalists this year).

The church bell tolls for a funeral; a frequent occurrence in the past year. Former vicars and past and present residents gather once again to pay their respects. The churchyard looks particularly tidy thanks to the efforts of Stuart Gregory and Professor Hugh Glanville. The evening ends with a Supporters of Allington and Boscombe Recreation Area Barn Dance and their coffers are swelled accordingly The last dog walker returns down the track to the ford wondering whether the Bourne will rise again before the millennium.

Jake Sturgess, aged 11

I have lived in Wiltshire all my life. I live in Melksham in a small cottage down Snarlton Lane. I do not know if it will still be there when you read this but that is where I lived when I was 11.

My favourite sports are tennis, football, cricket and golf! There is a high animal population and the countryside is endless. There are quite a few tourist attractions e.g. Stonehenge, that people from all over the world come to see! Also there is Avebury Stone Circles. They are hundreds of stones situated in a circle!

Kay Taylor

Do you really want to bury yourselves in a sleepy rural village, there'll be nothing to do and nothing ever happens? This is the question we were continually asked when my husband Alan's employers relocated to Wiltshire.

We had decided to take the plunge and move to a village rather than a town. After all, if we were leaving London we might as well go the whole hog - despite the fact that I was pregnant and couldn't drive. Our daughter Lucy arrived in 1976, and I passed my driving test in 1978. But, and there is always a 'but' when moving, the builders went bankrupt, which resulted in an eighteen-month delay in getting into our new home. However we finally moved to Sutton Benger in January 1978 and our son Ben arrived ten months later to complete our family – a villager born and bred.

The 1970s were a period of rapid growth for Sutton Benger, with the Chestnut Road estate virtually doubling the size of the village. The teething troubles of a new community of 'professionals' trying to integrate into a rural village had subsided by the time we arrived, the influx of the early settlers' children ensuring the survival of the village school. In 1974 parents formed the Friends of Sutton Benger School to raise funds for

---

Life at the turn of the century

additional facilities, and the group has just celebrated its silver anniversary. The W.I. was also re-established in 1974, bringing together women from the old and the new village.

In October 1978 the Mother, Baby & Toddler Group was set up, followed by the Playgroup in January 1979. Both groups have thrived although they now attract some of their members from outside the village, and – a sign of the politically correct times – the Toddler Group is now officially the Parent, Baby & Toddler Group.

Over the years the two halves of the village have become more united although some true villagers are still wary of accepting you to full village membership after a mere twenty years. Even so, involvement in village life counts for more than years of residency and I think I am almost accepted now. Since tentatively agreeing to be treasurer of the Toddler Group in 1979, I have been on committees for most of the village organisations: as vice-chair of Playgroup; a Friend of the School; W.I. president and captain of the scrabble team; a Neighbourhood Watch co-ordinator; a founder member of the Green Buttons Theatre Company; on the church door rota; and as a parish councillor since 1987, serving as chairman from 1991-94. I am also a trustee of a local charity, and village historian, as well as being the village correspondent for the *Wiltshire Gazette & Herald* and the contact for the BBC local radio station.

I wouldn't live anywhere else, but don't let anyone tell you that there is nothing to do in the country – say yes once and you're on committees for life.

James Thompson, age 13

● ●

When I arrived at a fantastic old mansion, with a lovely setting and scenery, I had doubts in my mind like; the children at the resort might be posh. I won't fit in, and I would suffer in work because I had come from a poor background and I was taught in a pretty bad school (in educational terms).

Surprisingly enough I realised I have great friends, I've finally settled in after a few drawbacks and I'm getting excellent grades. I have finally got into a routine after one year of being here. At 6.45 in the morning I wake up, rush to the showers competing with my friends and get ready for breakfast at seven thirty. There are a few things which I find annoying and they are: that the third years play awful music which gives most people headaches, also the grease on the eggs and the fat on the bacon.

I only live thirteen miles away so I go home every weekend which is really good as I can get a sample of both worlds, one being with my friends at the manor and two my friends at home in Pewsey. I find I am very fortunate to be in a fantastic school with great friends who look after me when I'm down and the great facilities such as a golf course, tennis courts, bicycle track and a volleyball net, which can also be used as a badminton net.

Sarah Tibbetts, age 13

At the moment I live in a small village in Wiltshire called Upton Lovell. I have lived there all my life. It is peaceful and everybody knows everybody else. You feel safe walking down the road with everyone looking out for you. There are no shops in our village, just a church, pub, and about seventy houses.

The nearest town is about eight miles away, but for all I know, in a few years that could all have changed and it could have crept right up to our doorstep. The towns are growing, along with crime and pollution. The environment is being damaged and there isn't a lot that people like me can do about it.

As we drive through the village I see ugly satellite dishes pinned up on the side of houses. Sky and cable are popular with the public - all those tele-addicts out there who love sitting in front of the television flicking through the two hundred channels like robots. It is a bit like my sister who spends all her time on the telephone chatting to her mates. Maybe, in the future she will be able to communicate in other ways as well. Such as being able to see as well as hear them using the T.V. or computer.

However this isn't relevant at the moment. My life is generally quiet in the tiny Wiltshire village. There are only about seven teenagers in the whole village. Most of the people are over fifty but there are also quite a few under five's. We seven all find that there is never anything for us to do. We don't really know each other very well since we all left the local primary school. We went our different ways to different schools further away and I find it hard even to remember their names sometimes.

I now go to Dauntsey's School in West Lavington. It takes about twenty minutes to drive there. The school day is long starting at 8.20am, finishing at 5.20pm, but I have made lots of friends there. All of my friends from school live miles away so I don't get to see them much out of school. I often find myself wandering around the house with nothing to do, and I think about what life could be like in the 21st century. I see the future as one big bubble of technology.

Gemma Tyler, age 15

I still marvel at every rabbit that I see hopping through fallow pastures, dancing in the morning gleam of sunlight which rhythmically flickers over scattered stray blades of grass — left there by the tractor. I still smile at the foals performing their self-choreographic dressages around their paddocks; I chuckled as they cower down in the cowslip and cerise thistles because an inquisitive sparrow had startled them. The vibrant pigments in the plumage of pheasants rummaging in the leafy hedgerows seize my eye even now: rusts and terracottas as rich as bronze; vivid fir reds and metallic laurel-greens that boast natural beauty. Even the plants are as stunning and graceful as I first recall: abundances of buttercups and dandelions like saffron stars in a sky of green; the posies of daffodils and poppies with their distinctive posture, standing tall to greet you in all their glory and frankness.

The busy streets contrast with the tranquil, rustic countryside: there are few stimulating colours — mostly greys dominate these urban areas; there is a constant buzz as people go about their daily business like ants streaming through their kingdoms; and life is all action: time is of the essence! As our bus trundles along its usual track at the same time each weekday, I am able to recognise those who are strangers — certain faces in the crowds become familiar as we pass so often — yet they would not know me sitting high up, gazing down, watching, I notice the things that to others are so normal: irregular trees, different adverts up on bill boards, cross-breeds of birds and the new signs now held by lollipop ladies. It is when I get off the bus at the end of the journey, however, that I become part of the 'normal', then, things do not seem so different.

Mrs Vera Tyler

Morning milking is over and I see our herd of Friesians leaving the farmyard 150 yards from the road. My CB crackles. "Cows coming, turn them up the lane please." I hurry out to the road, shutting my garden gate on the way, and wave down the traffic. Some drivers stop willingly, some are resentful, and the odd one is abusive. Road rage exists even on these country roads! My husband and son are following the cows in the farm truck. We shut the field gate and acknowledge the waiting drivers. I return to my kitchen.

On this glorious morning in mid-July the view from my kitchen window is spectacular. The hills in the distance with grazing sheep and cattle and, lower down, fields of wheat on the verge of turning into that wonderful gold. Nearer to home, barley, already with heads bent, waiting for the combine. I wonder if we will start ours today. If we do it'll be 'meals in the fields', so I set about making a batch of meat pasties and cakes, and bake them in my ever-faithful Aga.

The milk tanker rumbles by and turns into the farm. The driver will take a daily sample and pump the milk from our refrigerated tanks. The price of milk to the farmer constantly falls. Last month we were paid 18p per litre.

My CB crackles again. "We're starting the barley, can you bring out some lunch about one o'clock?" Thank goodness for the baking session. I put together the goodies and fill the big flask with home-made elderflower cordial. I see the combine trundle out of the shed bound for

---

its first work of the season. It's an old machine, but well maintained – fingers crossed it will see us through another harvest.

In the field I meet my daughter-in-law, bringing a lunch box for her husband and we discuss the crop. "Its coming off at 14% moisture," she says, so thankfully no drying to add extra expense. The current price is £71.00 per ton off the field. Five years ago it was round £90.00.

The phone rings. Our local agriculture dealer has a trailer part ready for collection. On the way there I meet our three granddaughters coming to help get the cows in for afternoon milking. Born into this farming life, at twelve, eleven and seven years, they are quite capable of playing their part.

Tea-time, and back to the field with more food, all is going well, sun shining, combine humming healthily, and a good crop.

I spend the evening making gooseberry jam. At 9 p.m. I hear the combine coming home and from my kitchen window see the sun setting a brilliant red, promising another good combining day tomorrow.

There is a general slump in farming but it's still a satisfying life, and one that we should be hard-pushed to quit.

Fiona Waite, age 10

I have lived in Wiltshire all my life. I like the countryside. The people are really nice and friendly. There are lots of places to visit such as Stonehenge and Avebury, all of which include historic stones.

I have two friends called Gemma Tasker and Chloe Beattie. I have one dog called Holly, one cat called Smokey and one rabbit called Pipa.

I visit my dad every fortnight in Swindon. I don't like it much there because there is not much countryside and the people are sly!

These songs are my favourite but they will probably be different to the songs you will have in your time: Britney Spears, 'Sometimes'; Vengaboys, 'Boom, Boom, Boom, Boom'

I go to Forest and Sandridge School in Melksham. It is a really nice school I have never changed schools! When I leave this school I will be going to Matravers in Westbury. It is a lovely school and I am sure I will enjoy it!

My name is Zara Ward, I live in the northern part of Wiltshire in a village called Brinkworth. I am eleven years-old, I was born in 1987 on October 14th.

I go to Brinkworth Earl Danbys Primary School, which is in my village. I catch the bus to school everyday, apart from weekends when I don't go to school. At school we have a playtime outside until 8.45 am when school starts. We have three playtimes – one first thing, one at 10.30 a.m. and one after lunch, at 12.30 p.m. School ends at 3.15 p.m. My school has got two sites, one site has the first two younger classes and the other site has the three older classes. In my school there are about 130 people, about 35 at one site and 95 people at the other. Altogether there are five classes and each class contains an average of 30 people but in my class there is 35 people (it is the largest class in the school) and I am in the top year, Year Six. My mum works as a support assistant at my school (not in my class, in the younger classes). At school I have a group of four friends.

I go to Guides every Tuesday, which is a social event organised by leaders. My favourite sports are netball and running, we have a netball team at school and we have a sports day, one day a year, which is great fun. We have lots of different races e.g. skipping, sprint, slow bicycle, bucket and ball, bunny rabbit and lots more.

In September I am going to secondary school in Malmesbury which isn't far away. I am looking forward to it.

My favourite meal is an English breakfast, which consists of eggs, bacon, beans and bread. My mum's boyfriend owns a farm and has got lots of animals – cows, sheep, ducks, pigs, turkeys and lots more, so we get fresh eggs from there: my sister, brother and I get the eggs from the chicken hut.

My mum and dad are divorced and my dad lives in Purton, which is about 15 minutes away. My dad is married again to a lady called Krys. My dad and Krys have had a baby together called Brittany, she is very sweet. I see my dad, Krys and Brittany every Wednesday and every other weekend.

For the millennium my family and I are planning to go to Dubai (in the Middle East) to see my auntie and her fiancé (they have moved there for three years).

I like my life in Wiltshire, there are lots of things to do, I really like it.

The village of Chilmark, in the south-west corner of Wiltshire, winds its way through the years like its Winterbourne stream: hardly seeming to exist for much of the year but burbling in gentle spate when excitement overtakes it in the form of a burglary or the recent Post Office fire.

On the face of it, it has hardly changed since the Great Fire of London in the 17th century produced the boom in stone quarrying which allowed the local stonemasons to build their fine cottages along The Street.

They stand now, grey and not pristine cream, but desirable residences still for all that. The Street is tarmaced now, of course, but it still bends, bordering the Winterbourne and throwing little wooden bridges over the summer-absent stream. The population has hardly changed in ninety years: 411 in 1901 and 425 in 1991. Why, the underground stone quarry first opened by the Romans two thousand years ago is still being mined! It provided sandy limestone for Salisbury cathedral in 1220 and for the rebuilding of Windsor Castle in 1992.

There have been changes, of course. The population is almost certainly older now, with the cottages extended to provide much-envied homes for folk who have retired rather earlier than their forebears. Boasting four pubs within living memory, the number is now reduced to the Black Dog, which has managed to pull off the difficult feat of remaining a home to the local pint drinkers while providing high quality food to a wide catchment area.

Surprisingly, cars are not everywhere. Virtually all villagers have them, of course, but they are, somehow, tucked away so that street parking is rare and only the occasional monstrous articulated rumbler reminds us of the existence of the A303, just two miles away. Sometimes, as young girls on ponies clip through the lanes in summer, it seems as though time has stood still.

It would be wrong, however, to portray Chilmark as God's Waiting Room. New low cost housing is about to be erected on the edge of the village to provide homes for younger people and the Chilmark and Fonthill

Bishop First School, sitting grey-square on the Street, bubbles with life and gets consistently good OFSTED reports. Children skate-board down Barnes Hill and the nearby Nadder provides challenging fishing for local lads as, more legitimately, it does for retired colonels.

It has to be admitted, though, that much of the social life of the village at this millennium end centres around the middle aged and older. A recent performance of CADS (the Chilmark Amateur Dramatic Society) featured, in review, a High Court judge, a Rear Admiral and the wife of a retired Bishop. The Dog, at most lunch-times has to listen, whether it likes it or not, to the pipe-swathed opinions of a cadre of regulars whose total age would frighten the most hardened insurance assessor.

Perhaps it was ever thus – at the last millennium, when the village knew the Danes and seventy years later when the Conqueror put the place in his Domesday Book; in 1588 when beacons were lit to warn of the Armada; during the Napoleonic threat when recruiting drums were heard on the Street; or at D Day, when, overnight, the village miraculously lost its friendly Yankee lodgers. Nothing really seems to change in Chilmark. It's that sort of village.

Evelyn Williams

The Village of Crudwell lies four miles north of Malmesbury and two miles from the Gloucestershire border. It is intersected by the A419 Malmesbury to Cirencester road, while the hamlets of Eastcourt, Murcott, Quelfurlong, Pat Yat, West Crudwell, Chedglow and Chelworth circle the village and form the Parish of Crudwell.

It is a rural community with horses taking prominence over the one dairy farm and several arable farms. It is also in the commuter belt, with Kemble Station three miles to the North and with easy access to the M4 and M5.

The village has all the buildings expected of a traditional English village. A church, school, two pubs, two hotels, a working forge, a village hall and a village green and cricket team. All the buildings are in a good state of repair and are obviously cared for, and it is in the latter respect that the true heart of Crudwell is to be found. For this is a caring village and all age groups work together for the benefit of the people and the village itself.

The annual Strawberry Fayre and Craft market, held in July to raise money for the upkeep of the church, is one example of how the villagers work together. Contributions include the lending of garden furniture, baking American shortcake, waiting at table, endless washing up or acting as steward in the Church.

The Fayre is preceded in June by the 24 Hour Bike Ride, a village hall fundraising event. For the people of Crudwell built their own village hall, big enough for a badminton court, short mat bowls and indoor short tennis to be played on a regular weekly basis throughout the year. The 'Bike Ride' is a masterpiece of organisation and demonstrates the many talents in the village ranging from electrical skills to public relations. The prestige is so high that clubs and individual riders, from distant towns and villages, come to partake in the seven-mile circuit.

The young of the village are well catered for with the usual youth schemes and opportunities and, to encourage young peoples' musical talent, 'Bob's Concert' takes place every June. Although Bob died a few years ago his widow has continued to encourage the event where the young entertain the villagers by playing their various musical instruments to the delight of all. For those with singing aspirations there is The Music Makers. This group of primary school children sing at the monthly Church Family Service and perform at various events during the year.

Despite the distance to the nearest town and cinemas, boredom is not apparent in the village. Indeed, for the large retired population of the village there is no time for boredom. Everyone seems to have a role and plays it with great enthusiasm and, in case anyone has forgotten what is happening in the village the monthly *Courier* keeps everyone informed of past, present and future events. Typed, edited and produced by the village people it is the umbilical cord which unites and makes the vibrant village which is Crudwell.

Elizabeth Wilson

I live in an estate that has got a quite an awful reputation. Drugs, burglary, and badly behaved children are the norm. Quite a few of the tenants are single mothers who have never been married. I am a divorcée (I can't say that I am proud of that fact) forty-three year-old woman who has a son of nine years. I live in "geriatric corner" – I have affectionately christened myself thus as most of the mothers are much younger than I.

I wonder if they have ever thought about the circumstances if they had lived the same life, just a few short years ago. No husband, no job, no income – workhouse life beckoned, which, of course, would have included me – or would it? Living within a domestic violence household is just as common these days – however there are escape routes for the victims.

However, wives who were in the same situation would, most likely, not even have considered leaving. The thought of workhouse life was just as horrendous, women and children alike were rarely thought of as human beings. No financial benefits existed; if no money, no food and no home – literally. And, of course, family allowance was certainly not paid out. Why pay women to have children? After all, it was a woman's duty to bear children.

When my son was born, it was impossible to protect him and myself. My child was 'safe'; unfortunately I was not, and eventually I was admitted to the hospital for mentally ill people in Devizes.

It is a huge Victorian building and, of course, 'asylum' was the usual description around that time. It has now closed and a more modern hospital has taken its place. I was a patient for two months and when I left I went back to the same life prior to my stay in hospital. Again, just a few years ago it would have been a certainty that I would never have been allowed to go 'home', I would have lost my son and my freedom.

My son and myself wouldn't have the luxury of leaving my violent husband; we were thrown out of the family home. Even though the two of us spent some months in a hostel for the homeless in Trowbridge, we had help and support. We have never been treated as 'outcasts' unlike many of the poor souls in past times. The women of those past years would never believe that, in these days, houses with all 'mod cons' would be allocated to young, single mothers. Receiving money without any kind of work would never be understood. Fortunately our lives have improved.

So, here we are preparing for the millennium. None of us can predict our future or that of our children. For today, we must strife for self-respect, and honour those women whose lives must certainly have been unbearably hard and very sad.

David Yaun, age 10

I live in Wiltshire and I go to school in Wiltshire. It is a very nice school and on Monday evening a special letter came. My Mum was calm because she had read it already but I was excited about it. It said that I had won a prize in a writing competition. I never thought I would get a badge or anything from Young Writers, but I did. We didn't have much time to read it, and the next day I showed it to everyone else at school.

When I went to school the next day Mrs Walling said very well done. I have started my career and I went hyper but I calmed myself down. I might not get the top prize , but I will definitely be a published author, even though I am dyslexic and dyspraxic and so are my friends. I think at my old school people couldn't help me as well as this one because they weren't anyway. I think dyslexia is a talent, although it often makes things difficult. I have a vivid imagination, but sometimes writing down my thoughts isn't easy.

At this school we have lambs, cows and two guinea-pigs and also some doves. It is a very nice school. It is near Bath, in the country and only dyslexic and dyspraxic children can come. There are about thirty children in the school. I come to school by car with two other children who live near me. We live in Trowbridge and we have to go to school in Colerne so it is quite a long way. The journey is OK. We listen to music on Radio 1 and talk about school. Sometimes in my Dad's car we listen to GWR.

More books on Wiltshire from Ex Libris Press:

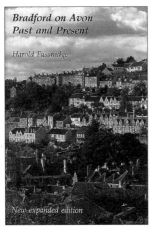

BRADFORD ON AVON: PAST AND PRESENT
by Harold Fassnidge
This updated edition remains the
standard history of the town
192 pages; Illustrated;
ISBN 0 948578 62 9; **Price £7.95**

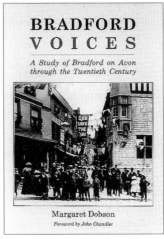

BRADFORD VOICES: *A Study of*
Bradford on Avon in the
Twentieth Century
by Margaret Dobson
256 pages; Illustrated;
ISBN 0 948578 89 0; **Price £9.95**

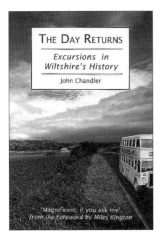

THE DAY RETURNS:
Excursions in Wiltshire's History
by John Chandler
This is the perfect dipping into book for
all lovers of Wiltshire.
256 pages; Illustrated
ISBN 0 948578 95 5
Price £9.95

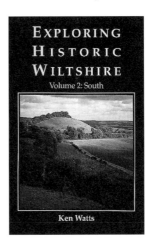

EXPLORING HISTORIC WILTSHIRE
Volume 2: South
by Ken Watts
Featuring six of the finest
landscapes of rural south Wiltshire.
176 pages; Illustrated
ISBN 0 948578 92 0 **Price £7.95**

THE LIMPLEY STOKE VALLEY
by Margaret Wilson
160 pages; Illustrated;
ISBN 0 948578 58 0; **Price £7.95**

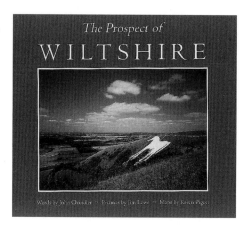

THE PROSPECT OF WILTSHIRE
Words by John Chandler;
Pictures by Jim Lowe
*112 pages; full colour maps and
photographs throughout;*
ISBN 0 948578 74 2; **Price £14.95**

A SENSE OF BELONGING
*History Community, and the
New Wiltshire*
by John Chandler
120 pages; Illustrated;
ISBN 0 948578 93 9; **Price £5.95**

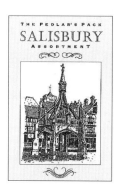

PEDLAR'S PACK:
A SALISBURY ASSORTMENT
Compiled by John Chandler
80 pages; Illustrated;
ISBN 0 948578 80 7; **Price £3.95**

*Ex Libris Press books are available through local bookshops or may
be obtained direct from the publisher, on receipt of net price, at*
1 The Shambles, Bradford on Avon, Wiltshire, BA15 1JS
Tel/fax 01225 863595   e-mail: rogjones37@hotmail.com
www.ex-librisbooks.co.uk